To our wives,
Cynthia J. Kellen-Yuen and Elizabeth Sheldon,
for their support and encouragement

Practical Grant Writing and Program Evaluation

FRANCIS K. O. YUEN
California State University, Sacramento

KENNETH L. TERAO
Aguirre International

DESK COPY

THOMSON
™
BROOKS/COLE

Australia • Canada • Mexico • Singapore • Spain • United Kingdom • United States

THOMSON

™

BROOKS/COLE

Executive Editior: *Lisa Gebo*
Assistant Editor: *Alma Dea Michelena*
Marketing Team: *Caroline Concilla and Mary Ho*
Signing Representative: *Marc Edwards*
Production Coordinator: *Mary Vezilich*
Production Service: *Buuji, Inc.*

Permissions Editor: *Sue Ewing*
Cover Designer: *Jennifer Mackres*
Compositor: *Buuji, Inc.*
Print Buyer: *Vena Dyer*
Printing & Binding: *Globus*

For more information about our products, contact us at:
Thomson Learning Academic Resource Center
1-800-423-0563

For permission to use material from this text, contact us by:
Phone: 1-800-730-2214   Fax: 1-800-730-2215
Web: http://www.thomsonrights.com

This publication is based on work supported for Project STAR by the Corporation for National and Community Service under Cooperative Agreement Nos. 99CACA0018 and 99CACA0002. Any opinions, findings, or conclusions or recommendations expressed in this book are those of Dr. Francis Yuen and Mr. Kenneth Terao. They do not reflect the views of the Corporation for National and Community Service.

Library of Congress Cataloging-in-Publication Data
Yuen, Francis K. O., [date].
    Practical grant writing and program evaluation /
Francis K.O. Yuen, Kenneth L. Terao.
        p. cm.
    Includes bibliographical references and index.
    ISBN-13: 978-0-534-54508-6
    ISBN-10: 0-534-54508-4

    1. Proposal writing in human services. 2. Social service. 3. Proposal writing for grants.
I. Terao, Kenneth L. II. Title.
HV41.2 .Y84 2002
658.15'224—dc21   2002018666

Brooks/Cole–Thomson Learning
511 Forest Lodge Rd.
Pacific Grove, CA 93950-5098
USA

Asia
Thomson Learning
5 Shenton Way #01-01
UIC Building
Singapore 068808

Australia
Nelson Thomson Learning
102 Dodds Street
South Melbourne, Victoria 3205
Australia

Canada
Nelson Thomson Learning
1120 Birchmount Road
Toronto, Ontario M1K 5G4
Canada

Europe/Middle East/Africa
Thomson Learning
High Holborn House
50/51 Bedford Row
London WC1R 4LR
United Kingdom

Latin America
Thomson Learning
Seneca, 53
Colonia Polanco
11560 Mexico D.F.
Mexico

Spain
Paraninfo Thomson Learning
Calle/Magallanes, 25
28015 Madrid, Spain

Contents

Chapter 4

Developing an Evaluation Plan   46

Chapter 5

The Strategies and Tools for Data Collection   61

Chapter 6

Data Analysis and Reporting   86

Chapter 7

Putting It Together: Model Program and Evaluation Plans   100

Chapter 8

Program Planning and Evaluation:
Practical Considerations and Implications   119

List of Boxes

Preface

It is our intention in this book to provide practical knowledge and skills for effective program planners and evaluators of human service programs. Program planning, grant writing, and program evaluation are presented with an emphasis on the interrelationship between these components and how each component enhances the others.

Outline of the Book

This book consists of eight chapters. The first chapter discusses the knowledge base necessary for program planning and program evaluation and their practical uses. Chapters two and three describe the program planning process and offer a general model for program planning. Included is a step-by-step guide to the grant writing process. In this way the reader can follow the strategies involved in program planning. We will use the federal Center for Substance Abuse Prevention (CSAP) and Center for Substance Abuse Treatment (CSAT) Demonstration Grant proposal development frameworks to provide readers with practical experience in preparing a detailed demonstration grant for human services. Readers will learn about the whole planning process from conceptualization to operationalized activities and tasks. Chapters four, five, and six describe the program evaluation process. The empowerment evaluation approach is emphasized, demonstrating how this approach supports the development and improvement of program services. Experience from various service projects will be utilized to explain the program evaluation process and its technology. These projects will include the Project STAR for the Corporation for National Service's AmeriCorps projects and the Save the Children Federation Inc., U.S. Community Partner Projects, as well as CSAP and CSAT demonstration projects. Readers will learn the development and the implementation of program evaluation plans, data collection and analyses, and report writing. Case examples including evaluation plans, data collection instruments, and report writing will be used. Chapter seven provides several examples of program and evaluation plans including ethical considerations and practice in program evaluation. Chapter eight discusses the implications of program planning and program evaluation for human service providers.

Acknowledgments

Francis Yuen is thankful for the teaching, support, and understanding of his families. Their wisdom and consideration made the completion of this book possible. Kenneth Terao is thankful to his parents for their support of his education, and their continued encouragement that helped him to coauthor this book.

The authors would like to thank Lisa Gebo and Alma Dea Michelena of Brooks/Cole for their support, flexibility, consideration, and patience throughout the development of this book. We appreciate the production and editorial support of Sara Dovre Wudali of Buuji, Inc., as well as the initial editorial assistance of Terry Brown. The authors also want to express their thanks to Lance Potter and Carol Hafford of the Corporation for National Service, Catherine Milton and Terry Russell of Save the Children Federation, Inc., and Aguirre International and the staff and coaches of Project STAR for their inspiration, encouragement critiques, and cooperation.

We would also like to thank our reviewers for their helpful suggestions: Lynn Atkinson, Tulsa Community College; John Gunther, Eastern Michigan University; Gwat-Yong Lie, University of Wisconsin, Milwaukee; Roland Meinert, President, Missouri Association for Social Welfare; John Pardeck, Southwest Missouri State University; Greg Skibinski, Southwest Missouri State University; Santos Torres, California State University, Sacramento.

Finally, we are indebted to the human service providers who have shared with us their insights, feedback, and guidance which have allowed us to shape our ideas and organize the information for this book.

Francis K. O. Yuen
Kenneth L. Terao

About the Authors

Francis K. O. Yuen is an associate professor for the Division of Social Work at California State University, Sacramento. He has many years of direct practice, program development, and management experience. In addition to being a program development and evaluation consultant for human service organizations and a Coach for Project STAR, he is also a grant proposal reviewer for various government agencies. He publishes and teaches on family health social work practice, substance abuse and high-risk behaviors, diversity, grant writing, and research and program evaluation.

Kenneth L. Terao is Vice President of Aguirre International, a social science research firm located in San Mateo, California. He has over 15 years of program management experience working in a variety of institutions and organizations, including elementary/secondary education, higher education, community organizations, law enforcement, and local government agencies. For the past 6 years, he has directed national evaluation projects funded by the Corporation for National Service (Project STAR) and Save the Children Federation, which provides training and technical assistance to local, state, and national organizations on developing and implementing outcome evaluations on community service projects.

RATIONALITY AND REALITY OF PROGRAM PLANNING AND EVALUATION

What is a program? What does it intend to achieve? What are the basic properties of planning and evaluation? How are they related? This chapter presents a basic understanding of the characteristics of program planning and program evaluation. Planning and evaluation are mostly goal-oriented activities that incorporate many linear-sequential and logical thinking procedures. They are also products of social, economic, and political realities, continuously evolving and moving in a spiral fashion. Successful planning and evaluation demand the arts of balance and inclusiveness of ideology and reality.

Defining Programs

A program is a coordinated change effort that is theory based, goal-oriented, often time limited, target population-specific, and activity driven. It is also an evolving process. A program is the result of some type of planning. Programs are intended to achieve particular goals with their special intervention approaches and operating procedures.

Mayer (1985) defines a program as "an intervention that constitutes a service or activity that can be provided to facilitate volitional change." He views planning as "the design of interventions" (p. 21). Royse, Thyer, Padgett, and Logan (2001) describe a program as "an organized collection of activities designed to reach certain objectives . . . a series of planned actions that are designed to solve some problem" (p. 5). Mika (1996) depicts a program as "a design of activities that, in theory, produce some change or outcome in its participants within a given time frame" (p. 6). Weinbach (1998) portrays a program as a "complex system"; a "self-contained package with its own goals, policies, procedures, and rules, and frequently its own budget" (p. 91).

In human service organizations, programs are often referred as "services." Each of these programs is supposed to bring the agency closer toward fulfilling its organizational mission. Ideally, all programs supplement and enhance one another. In reality, however, there may be overlapping, as well as competition, among programs for the limited resources available.

Fiscally, there are financially rich programs and there are, more often than not, poorly funded programs. Nevertheless, most of the funding for programs is earmarked for particular purposes and usages. When the agency administrations get too "creative" and start inappropriately and excessively commingling funding, or "robbing Peter to pay Paul," the integrity of the program will suffer. Subsequent discontent and disagreements from staff of different programs and their clients are among the critical reasons that can bring down a program.

Similarly, programs are supposed to be time limited. Many human service programs and organizations have outlived their original timeframes, functions, and purposes; however, they continue to exist. A possible situation of goal displacement might have occurred. The survival, continuation, and status quo of a program or organization become the goal of the entity, not meeting the needs of the clients it serves. Clients instead become the means, not the end. The survival goals replace the original service goals.

Beyond the general references of programs as coordinated human service interventions at the agency and community levels, there are "social programs" that are the implementations of particular social policies. Social programs are organized interventions that aim to improve a social situation that may be a social problem, a social need, or a condition that requires specific actions. Social programs could also be mandated through formal sanctions such as social policies. These social programs and their sponsoring agencies could be drastically different in size, scope, theoretical and philosophical foundations, practice approaches, mandates, and many other aspects. Social programs are carried out through a variety of specific plans and interventions that have particular services/components and activities.

There are no programs or social programs that are "cure all and for all" by addressing every aspect or need of a social condition. A grassroots public education campaign alone certainly cannot cure the disease of AIDS. It could, however, contribute to the better prevention and understanding of the disease in the target populations, and address specific aspects of needs and issues of this public health concern. Programs therefore should clearly communicate their service intentions by being specific in their scope and associated goals, objectives, activities, and outcomes. It is through program evaluation that the attainment of program goals and the quality of the program are assessed.

A program is inherently a planned process to achieve particular future goals. It is conceived through a careful process of planning and design to bring about the desired change. Good program planning is a necessary, though not sufficient, cause for a successful program. Subsequently, the effectiveness of the program—or the change that programs can actually produce—will not be clearly identified and documented if there is no program evaluation. Planning, implementation, and evaluation are the integral features of programs.

Rubin and Babbie (1997) cited Rossi and Freeman's (1982) discussion on the purpose of program evaluation. It is "to assess and improve the conceptualization, design, planning, administration, implementation, effectiveness, efficiency, and utility of social interventions and human service programs" (p. 547). Rubin and Babbie further assert that "much of what we call social work research could be called program evaluation research" (p. 545). This is because "program evaluation has more to do with the purposes of research than with specific research methods" (p. 547).

Program Planning and Program Evaluation: Two Sides of a Coin

"A program and evaluation of a program are not separate activities. When planned carefully, these two set of activities can be integrated into an organized set of ongoing operations that promote and support each other" (Mika, 1996, p. 6). Program planning is an organized process through which a set of coordinated activities or interventions is developed to address and facilitate change in some or all of the identified problems. It is an ongoing process of development with the intention of designing a set of activities that will tackle the identified needs and problems. Program planning is a means for program development. It is a goal-oriented activity based on the assessed needs or problems.

Program planning not only concerns what will happen, it also involves the assessment of what has happened and what really would have happened. It is by design and by its very nature related to needs assessment and program evaluation. Needs or problems assessment is the necessary and fundamental step for any successful program planning. These assessments provide the rationale and direction for the development of program plans. Once the program interventions are implemented, the performance and the attainment of intended objectives are then evaluated. Assessments represent the front end or the basic appraisals, and evaluations reflect the continuous reviews and judgments.

Kettner, Moroney, and Martin (1999) propose effectiveness-based program planning that "involves taking a program through a series of steps designed to produce a clear understanding of the problem to be addressed, to measure client problem type and severity at entry, to provide a relevant intervention, to measure client problem type and severity at exit, and to examine selected indicators in a follow-up study to determine long-range outcomes" (pp. 6–7). This type of program planning incorporates program evaluation throughout the process and provides continuous assessment of the program performance to gain further improvement.

In practice, funding sources are no longer willing to allocate resources for human services and expect merely a report on whether or not the program and service providers did what they said they would do. Funders want to know what benefits are gained from the services provided. Programs are now required to evaluate their services and show the results (process, outcome, and impact) of the services provided. Consequently, service providers must pay more attention to well developed program plans in order to ensure the highest probability of reaching and producing the desired results.

United Way of America (1996) discusses the difference between the Traditional Service Program model and the Program Outcome model. The traditional model basically includes inputs, activities, and outputs. "Inputs include resources dedicated to or consumed by the program" (p. 17). These resources involve a wide range of assets and investments such as money, staff time, facilities, equipment, and supplies. Regulations, mandates, and funding restraints are also part of the inputs. "Activities are what the program does with the inputs to fulfill its mission" (p. 17). They are the service methodologies such as interventions and strategies. "Outputs are the direct products of program activities and usually are measured in terms of volume of work accomplished" (p. 17). In this sense, the outputs are basically process data that testify what and how many activities have been done.

The preferred program outcome model adds an important component of "outcomes" at the end of the traditional program model. The outcome model includes inputs, activities, outputs, and outcomes. "Outcomes are benefits or change for individuals or populations during or after participating in program activities" (United Way of America, 1996, p. 18). Outcomes answer the basic question of "whether, and how much, a program's participants have changed, how their status has improved, how they have benefited" (p 18). The focus is beyond what has been done; it is on what changes or benefits have been produced after the participation in program activities. These changes or outcomes "may relate to behavior, skills, knowledge, attitudes, values, condition, status, or other attributes" (p. 18).

Whether it is the traditional or the outcome model, there remains the importance of careful and thoughtful assessment, planning, activity design and implementation, and evaluation of program results. Again, there is an interrelated and symbiotic relationship between planning and evaluation.

The Political Economy of Program Planning and Evaluation

Program evaluation supposedly provides useful information for improving the programs and the service delivery systems. In practice, many political and economic variables can make planning and evaluation undesirable and reluctant tasks. Program planning and evaluation are both the process and the product of the political and economic environments. Political economy is the interaction and dynamic between politics and economic interests. Netting, Kettner, and McMurtry (1999) state, "political means the process by which the organization obtains power and legitimacy. Economic means the process by which the organization gets resources such as clients, staff, and funding" (p. 219).

Many researchers (e.g., Grinnell, 1997; Rubin & Babbie, 1997) have discussed the various political and economic concerns about program evaluation. First, there are issues with the "political correctness" or "favoritism" of evaluations. Groups with competitive interests want to see the evaluation data work towards their favors, or be presented in ways so that all political bases are covered. They may use their political influence to "guide" the evaluation to present or not to present the "selected" truth.

Although scientific inquiries are supposed to be objective and unbiased, many people performing program evaluation tasks receive pressure to make the program look good. Program evaluation activities are often not among the highest priority for administrative and financial support. Consequently, individuals who have the program evaluation assignments may not be the ones who have the competency or commitment to carry out quality research procedures. The original purpose of describing the program as it is, and any improvement that should be made, could easily be replaced. In its place may be the nice and encouraging report that aims to secure current and future funding.

It is common among human service organizations to have in-house evaluators, although certain funding sources may require the use of external evaluators. There are pros and cons for having an internal or external evaluator. Internal evaluators may have better access and familiarity to the organization, staff, and information; they are also part of the organization. Internal politics, personal knowledge, and future plans within the organization may contribute to the less than desirable arrangement to have internal evaluators. External evaluators need time to get to know the organization, the program, and its politics. Meanwhile, staff members can also view them as outsiders that the administrators hire to "spy" on the staff. Whether they are internal or external evaluators, their ability to build trust with the program staff and to maintain independence, objectivity, and ethical and quality practice are among the most important considerations.

Not surprisingly, there are resistances from program staff and clients. Evaluation is perceived as an additional, undesirable, and labor-intensive assignment. It takes away the precious time that program staff and clients could use to provide or receive more direct service or activities. Developing buy-in from all levels within the organization is a major issue for any successful program evaluation task. The few useful approaches include involvement of concerned parties from the very beginning of the project, and providing useful reports on findings. These involvements have to be real and genuine participation. They include many activities; from conceiving the needs and outcomes of the program and its evaluation, to designing evaluation approaches and reporting findings. If staff find they have no time to do evaluation, the agency should be sure that there is built-in or allotted time to complete evaluation tasks.

Staff and clients are frustrated when they provide all the data demanded but never see the reports that come from those data. Even if they do see the reports, often those findings are outdated, not useable, or of no personal significance for them. Certainly, program evaluation reports need to be user friendly and useful to readers. Providing timely reports or feedback of the evaluation findings to the service users or people under study is an important piece of the evaluation puzzle.

The Technology of Program Planning and Program Evaluation

When we talk about technology, we may think it is about computers. Technology in human services, according to Lewis, Lewis, Packard, and Souflee (2001), is about "the transformation process" (p. 58). It is the transformation of inputs into outputs. Inputs are the resources such as data and information of needs and problems, intervention methods, and staffing. Outputs are the services and goods that are produced as the result of utilization of the inputs. Technology is involved in the service delivery model—the practice method that transforms resources or inputs into services or outputs that serve the clients and the community.

According to Germain (1983), technology is a professional values-guided application of theories, knowledge, and skills to practice. Germain further states that "approaches, methods, skills, and techniques are considered to make up technology" (p. 18). To understand technology, one must first distinguish among the often confusing terms: theory, knowledge, approaches, models, methods, skills, and techniques.

Reynolds (1971) notes that theory has been referred to as conceptualization, prescriptions for behaviors, or untested ideas. Yuen (1999b) defines theory as "a set of interrelated propositions or concepts, organized in some systematic manner, that offers an explanation of some phenomena" (p. 18).

Yuen (1999a) expands on Atherton and Klemmack's (1982) listing of four sources of knowledge: tradition, experience, common sense, and science. He explains that "tradition is custom and beliefs that have been handed down from generation to generation. It is not necessarily logical or rational, but it makes sense to the people who practice it. Experience is the person's first-hand observation" (p. 106). Sarcastically, everyone expects each other has a common sense and knows what a common sense is. Although in reality it is an odd and somewhat difficult term to define, "common sense is the combination of tradition and experience" (p. 106). Finally, "scientific knowledge is developed mainly through logical and rational validations. It is not the source of absolute knowledge, but it provides the objective means of knowing in addition to the other more subjective ways of knowing" (pp. 106–107).

These many ways of knowing lead to the establishment of certain knowledge, which, according to Germain (1983), forms a "recognizable or recognized perspective entities often called practice model" or approach (p. 31). Method is the specific application of such a model or approach with specific target groups. Germain notes that skill refers to a "particular area of practitioner action, such as observation, engagement, data collection, assessment, contracting, setting goals and planning, and achieving goals. Technique is used to designate a more specific procedure within such an area of skill" (p. 31). Technology is therefore the combination and application of the theories, knowledge, approaches, methods, skills, and techniques that produce the services.

Program planning could be considered as the selection and decision-making effort that attempts to identify and develop the finest service model. Ideally, this is a model that best utilizes the resources and would achieve the most desirable results. Paralleled with the program planning process and the actual implementation of services is the program evaluation process. The program evaluation provides both the formative and summative data that could be used to measure and assess the desirability and quality of the plan and its program.

Many factors contribute to the development of new service programs. Agency staff's observations and experience of working with the target population certainly generate internal impetus for the development of new programs. Similarly, social and political factors including legislations and government policies could mandate the development of new services. Needs assessment is an objective way to identify and characterize needs and accordingly develop appropriate services. Once an agency identifies the needs and conceptualizes the program ideas, the work of developing program goals, objectives, and activities begins, in order to define the scope and the results of the program. A set of well defined goals and objectives also provides the base for program monitoring and evaluation. Logic model and goal attainment scale are examples of some of the commonly used program development tools. Chapter 3 discusses the logic model in greater detail.

Program evaluation is the application of different social research designs in assessing the needs and results of programs. Evaluative research utilizes various research designs including exploratory, descriptive, and experimental designs. The exploratory study is designed to gain familiarity and develop hypotheses regarding a particular topic. It is achieved through methods (Atherton & Klemmack, 1982) such as:

1. Literature survey and documentary study
2. Experience study and historical study
3. Study of selected examples, typical cases, and extreme cases
4. Interview with individuals with different viewpoints
5. Review of one's experience and self-report

Descriptive research provides "description of a phenomenon or the description of the relationships between two or more phenomena" (Atherton & Klemmack, 1982, p. 29). It has a clear statement of problem and is more precise in its data collection, possibly involving sampling. Descriptive research therefore is designed to:

1. Describe some characteristics of the program, the service recipients, and other elements.
2. Describe the use of community resources, facilities, and other resources.
3. Solicit people's views on an issue.
4. Study the relationship of association among various variables/factors.

Needs assessment, for example, is a commonly used exploratory or descriptive study. Some descriptive research designs involve the use of hypothesis. A hypothesis is an educated guess and a statement that can be tested in an empirical way. It defines the relationship of one or more concepts so that the relationship can be tested. Although both a hypothesis and an assumption are one's hunch or speculation, they direct very different outcomes. When a person has a hypothesis of a certain situation, he or she will proceed with a scientific inquiry to test the hypothesis that may or may not generate conclusive answers. However, when a person is operating on an assumption, the person already has a preconceived notion or the answer for the identified situation. He or she will proceed as if the answer is true and that testing is not required. The only question is how true his or her assumption is, but not whether it is true.

In many situations, program planners operate on assumptions that are informed by professional literature, relevant data, and people's experiences. These assumptions will form the orientations and the basic service models of the proposed intervention program and become the program philosophy. Program evaluation, meanwhile, provides the needed validation and checking of this philosophy and its operations. In order for the program implementation and evaluation people to know what they should do to objectively assess program success and failure, specific working program hypotheses are formed and used to guide the implementation and evaluation processes. Atherton and Klemmack (1982) discuss the different hypotheses in descriptive research:

1. X has a particular attribute or characteristic such as "Children who have positive adult role models in their lives tend to have better success in schools."
2. X happens more often than Y in a given population, such as "Limited employment opportunities that pay a living wage occur more frequently than the lack of vocation training in single parents who are on welfare."
3. X is substantially associated with Y, such as "The more frequent presence of resilient factors, the less likely the youth will engage in high-risk behaviors."

Experimental research anticipates causality, in so far as this is possible, as well as association. It involves:

1. Independent variable (X) and dependent variable (Y): change in Y depends on change in X, or change in X will bring about change in Y.
2. Experimental group (the group that receives intervention/administration of the independent variable) and control group (the group that does not receive intervention).

Atherton and Kelmmack (1982) further discuss the contributory, contingent, and alternative hypotheses in experimental research.

1. Contributory: X is one of the factors that changes the likelihood of Y, such as "Hard work increases the likelihood of getting good grades."
2. Contingent: Under certain situation and predicament, X may be culpable for the likelihood of change in Y, such as "Job placement services will decrease the number of people who are on the welfare roll, when the economy is doing well."
3. Alternative: Either X or Z alters the likelihood of Y, such as "Changes in either parents' or their children's behaviors will lead to fewer child abuse incidents."

Box 1.1 provides a brief review of various experimental designs.

Summary

Program planning and evaluation should be the integral parts of any programs. This chapter provides the basic understanding of program planning and program evaluation. It emphasizes that planning and evaluation are products of rational thinking as well as political and economical considerations. The technology of planning and evaluation explains how it incorporates different types of knowledge and is carried out in a range of basic designs with various working hypotheses and assumptions.

References

Atherton, C., & Klemmack, D. (1982). *Research methods in social work.* Lexington, MA: D.C. Heath.

Germain, C. (1983). Technological advances. In A. Rosenblatt & D. Waldfogel (Eds.), *Handbook of clinical social work* (pp. 26–57). San Francisco: Jossey-Bass.

Grinnell, R. (1997). *Social work research and evaluation: Quantitative and qualitative approaches.* Itasca, IL: P.E. Peacock.

Kettner, P., Moroney, R., & Martin, L. (1999). *Designing and managing programs: An effectiveness-based approach* (2nd ed.). Thousand Oaks, CA: Sage.

Lewis, J., Lewis, M., Packard, T., & Souflee, F. (2001). *Management of human service programs* (3rd ed.). Belmont, CA: Brooks/Cole.

> **BOX**
> **1.1**   EXAMPLES OF EXPERIMENTAL DESIGNS

X: Administration of the independent variable
O: Observation of measurement of the dependent variable
R: Random assignment

A. Preexperimental Designs
   1. The one-shot case study / cross-sectional case study
                        X   O

   2. The one-group pretest-posttest
            O1   X   O2

   3. The static group comparison
                        X   O   (experimental group)
                                 O   (control group)

B. True Experimental Designs
   1. Cross-sectional survey
            R   X   O

   2. The pretest-posttest control-group design
        R   O1   X   O2
        R   O1   O2

   3. The posttest-only control-group design
        R   X   O
        R   O

   4. The Solomon four-group design
        R   O   X   O
        R   O   O
        R   X   O
        R   O

C. Quasiexperimental Designs
   1. The nonequivalent comparison group
            O1   X   O2
            O1   O2

   2. The time-series quasiexperimental design—interrupted time series
        O1   O2   O3   O4   X   O5   O6   O7   O8

   3. The multiple time-series design
        O1   O2   O3   O4   X   O5   O6   O7   O8
        O1   O2   O3   O4   O5   O6   O7   O8

   4. The single-subject design or the single-case study: A (Baseline), B (Intervention).
        AB
        ABAB

Mayer, R. (1985). *Policy and program planning: A developmental perspective.* Englewood Cliffs, NJ: Prentice Hall.

Mika, K. (1996). *Program outcome evaluation: A step-by-step handbook.* Milwaukee, WI: Families International, Inc.

Netting, E., Kettner, P., & McMurtry, S. (1999). *Social work macro practice.* (2nd ed.). New York: Longman.

Office for Substance Abuse Prevention. (1992). *Three management tools for OSAP Demonstration projects for pregnant and postpartum women and their infants (PPWI): Logic models, GOAMs charts, and evaluation plans.* Rockville, MD: Alcohol, Drug Abuse, and Mental Health Administration.

Reynolds, P. (1971). *A primer in theory construction.* Indianapolis: Bobbs-Merrill.

Royse, D., Thyer, B., Padgett, D., & Logan, T. (2001). *Program evaluation: An introduction* (3rd ed.). Belmont, CA: Brooks/Cole.

Rubin, A., & Babbie, E. (1997). *Research methods for social work* (3rd ed.). Pacific Grove, CA: Brooks/Cole.

United Way of America (1996). *Measuring program outcomes: A practical approach.* Alexandria, VA: Author.

Weinbach, R. (1998). *The social worker as manager: A practical guide to success.* (3rd ed.). Needham Heights, MA: Allyn & Bacon.

Yuen, F. K. O. (1999a). Family health and cultural diversity. In J. T. Pardeck & F. K. O. Yuen (Eds.), *Family health: A holistic approach to social work practice* (pp. 101–113). Westport, CT: Auburn House.

Yuen, F. K. O. (1999b). The properties of family health approach. In J. T. Pardeck & F. K. O. Yuen (Eds.), *Family health: A holistic approach to social work practice* (pp. 17–28). Westport, CT: Auburn House.

Planning, Evaluating, and Grant Writing

Knowing where you are and what you need are among the most important initial tasks of a successful program planning process. From conducting needs assessments to a simple program planning approach, this chapter will discuss the fundamental tasks for effective program planning and evaluation. Essentially, the program planning process is similar to that of writing a well-developed grant proposal. Readers will learn about effective grant writing processes and techniques in this and the following chapters.

Grant and Contract

There is often confusion about the difference between the terms *grant* and *contract*. Coley and Scheinberg (1990) point out that "a grant is a sum of money given to an agency or individual to address a problem or need in the community," whereas "a contract is a legal agreement that specifies the service to be provided and the results expected in exchange for resources" (p. 13).

A funding source may agree to provide $500,000 to fund a 2-year comprehensive homeless family intervention program proposed by a social service agency. At the end of the grant funding in 2 years, the agency has to seek out new funding to support the program if it chooses to continue the program. Grant funding is awarded to start new programs, not the continuation of old programs. Meanwhile, the agency may also have a service contract with the county social service department to provide 6,000 units of mental health counseling service and 500 housing referrals for at least 300 homeless families annually. There will be a contract renegotiation at the end of each fiscal year to adjust the cost and the service volume, or even the service contents. In most situations, if the contractual services have been satisfactorily delivered and the need continue to exist, the services will continue with the new contract.

The difference between grant and contract is similar to that between stipend and salary. If a person receives a stipend or scholarship, he or she is sponsored and encouraged by the funding source to engage in certain pursuits that are of interest to both parties. This sponsorship is time limited. On the other hand, if a staff person receives a salary, he or she would have an employment contract, or be on the basis of contract-at-will, to perform specific tasks or functions within a particular job title. In return for his or her service, the employer would provide an agreed upon salary with benefits. This employment contract presumably keeps going as long as the employment conditions continue to be favorable.

Program Planning and Grant Writing

A program planning process involves the development and use of activities, such as setting up goals, objectives, activities, and evaluation. This process presents the logic and the argument that justify the need, the significance, and the relevance of the proposed plan. A grant proposal is a written program plan that is specifically developed to gain financial assistance from a funding source to support the proposed services. Program planning provides the process and the framework for the development of a service grant proposal. Grant proposal is a specific type of product of program planning. Both of them involve logical thinking and are objective driven. They also take into considerations of the political economy surrounding the funding source and the problem to be addressed.

Among the concerns for good program planning and grant writing are the understanding and involvement of the target population. It is not uncommon for a human service agency to assign the planning or grant writing functions to one of its managerial staff or to a contracted planner or grant writer. Proceeding from the usual deductive ways of planning and based on the available data and theoretical frameworks, these planners and grant writers develop their plans or proposals on their own. What is missing in this process is input from the target population. Such solicitation not only increases the quality of the program plan but also allows the opportunity to develop the very important "buy-in" from the target population.

A Simple Formula for Program Planning

Many are familiar with the usage of terms such as *what, why,* and *how* in making plans. By using this common strategy, one can easily map out the basic concerns in developing any plan. Based on this common approach, a program planning formula is developed to guide a comprehensive planning process (see Box 2.1).

Program planning is an ongoing and dynamic process. It is also consistent with systems theory; that the whole is greater than the sum of its parts. Program planning is not merely a sum of all the planning components; it is a dynamic process that is the result of the interplay (multiplications) of its various components. The planning product itself is more than a combination of its parts.

Imagine that Mary goes to school every day with a stop at her parents' home in order to drop off her children for daycare. If there are only two ways (A and B) to go from Mary's house to her parents' house, and there are only three ways (C, D, and E) from her parents' house to the school, how many possible routes are there for Mary to go to school? As one may suspect, the answer is not five (A, B, C, D, and E). The correct answer is not the sum of the available ways. In fact, there are six ways to go from home to school with a stop at Mary's parents. The answer of six represents AC, AD, AE, BC, BD, and BE. Mathematically, it is two ways multiplied by three ways ($2 \times 3 = 6$). Similarly, program planning is not the five Ws plus two Hs plus one E; it is the multiplications of all these variables. The multiplications represent the many interactive outcomes that involve the interplay of the many components. Program planning is not strictly a straightforward and linear-sequential process. Instead, it is a spiral process that involves the back and forth, as well as the ups and downs, of the interactions among components as it moves forward.

The first W that concerns any planner is the "why." It is both the reason and the aim for the planning process. As a reason, it represents the needs and problems that bring about the desire for a program plan. As an aim, it defines the goals and objectives for the program plan to achieve. Program persons who do not understand the reasons for their program's existence and the goals that they should achieve tend to be confused and lack accomplishments. On the other hand, program persons who fixate on the "why," while their program lacks actual interventions or actions, tend to have plenty of empty promises and lack concrete outcomes.

BOX 2.1 **PROGRAM PLANNING FORMULA**

$P^2 = W^5 \times H^2 \times E$

Whereas,

- P^2 = <u>P</u>rogram <u>P</u>lanning
- W^5 = <u>W</u>hy x <u>W</u>ho/Whom x <u>W</u>hen x <u>W</u>here x <u>W</u>hat
- H^2 = <u>H</u>ow x <u>H</u>ow much
- E = <u>E</u>valuation

"Who" represents the target population that the program plan intends to serve. It also comprises the "whom"—by whom will these activities be implemented—the staff, the volunteers, and the cooperative organizations. A good program plan should have a clear understanding and description of its target population. This understanding includes the needs and problems of the target populations, their characteristics, and their environments. It enables the development and employment of culturally competent accesses to reach the population. This program plan should also contain the design or the composition of program staff to support the proposed services. These include both the qualification and quality of the program staff, as well as the staff management plan.

The "when," "where," and "what" are the logistics of the program. They are more than the implementation details. Timing and duration of programs—"when"—are essential to the success of the program. "Where" is about location and the accessibility of the program to the target populations. "What" represents the equipments and supply that the program needs to achieve its goals.

The two H's represent "how" and "how much." "How" is delineation of the service delivery systems and their activities. The means through which the intended services are provided to meet the identified needs or objectives. "How much" is the "$64,000 question" of program budgeting. It involves not only how much money, but also how the organization allocates and uses the funds. In fact, it is by itself a program plan for the money and resources. It is a fiscal program plan that goes with the service program plan.

Finally, the E is the evaluation. How do service providers, service recipients, and the funding source know the extent that the program has achieved its objectives? If so, how well? Furthermore, what kinds of impact might it have?

Needs Assessments and Other Preplanning Considerations

Many people consider needs assessment as a form of evaluation and techniques that are used at the beginning of any program planning process. It provides the necessary data to guide the development of the program plan. "A needs assessment describes the target population or community, including demographic characteristics, the extent of relevant problems or issues of concern, and current services" (Lewis, Lewis, Packard, & Souflee, 2001, p. 31). Mayer (1985) defines needs assessment as "the difference between the extent of a condition or need in a given population and the amount of service provided to meet that need" (p. 127).

What is a need? Mayer (1985) reports Bradshaw's (1977) discussions of four types of needs: normative, felt, expressed, and comparative. *Normative need* refers to certain conditions that are below the established social standards. Examples are family income that falls below the national or local poverty line and students whose low family incomes qualify them for free school meals. *Felt need* refers to the want based on the individual's standards. Depending upon their conditions and functioning, individuals may request to have different types of services they desire. A homeless mother and her two children normatively are in need of stable housing. She may also want housing in a particular neighborhood so she can walk to her work and drop off her children to a relative for care.

Expressed need refers to attempts by the individuals to fulfill their needs. Individuals such as the aforementioned homeless mother placing names of her family members on the waiting list for Title 8 housing assistance formulates the expressed need. Collectively, they become the service demand. *Comparative need* refers to the situation that an individual's condition is relatively worse off or less desirable than that of other people. The fact that this homeless mother's two children have more infectious disease-related emergency room visits than children their ages who live in a stable home reflects the comparative need and urgency for better care for the homeless families.

Rubin and Babbie (1997, p. 570) list several categories of needs assessment: (a) the key informants approach, (b) the community forum approach, (c) the rates-under-treatment approach, (d) the social indicators approach, (e) the community survey approach, and (f) the focus group approach. All of these approaches have their own advantages and pitfalls. Program planners may need to use more than one approach to gain a comprehensive or representative understanding.

Key informants are individuals who have special knowledge about the identified issues. They range from the service providers to the service recipients and their caregivers. Through the use of interviews and questionnaires, their special insights and comments regarding the situations will be collected.

Community forums such as open forums or town hall meetings provide a channel for concerned citizens to express and exchange their opinions.

Rates-under-treatment refers to the estimate of future service needs based on the current client data, including service usages and the waiting list. This approach can be carried out by doing documentary studies of existing or secondary data.

The *social indicators* approach utilizes the existing statistics and markers to study the condition of the target population. School dropout rate, infant mortality rate, and child abuse reports are examples of such an approach.

Survey of communities or target groups involves the use of both qualitative and quantitative research approaches to gather information directly from the target populations.

Finally, *focus groups* are usually made up of 12 to 15 people who represent the intended target population. Through a set of guided focus group questions, they provide thoughtful responses to the topics. Additionally, the group discussions and dynamics also bring about new ideas and discussions that the planners have not thought about.

Quantitative and Qualitative Approaches

Part of the misunderstanding of program evaluation and social research is that evaluation and research is all about numbers. Many believe that when using numbers, they apply statistics and a quantitative way of dealing. Furthermore, when statistics are involved, program evaluation is thought to be for science-minded people such as mathematicians, statisticians, or program evaluators. Some human service providers may argue they should concentrate on what they do best, such as dealing with people and improving their well being. They are better trained and capable in more qualitative domains and should let the evaluators or managers deal with the headaches of scientific evaluation. Certainly, there are many faults in the logic just described. Nevertheless, they reflect the resistance and misunderstanding among many human service providers who believe they are "people people" not "science people"; that they should not be concerned about, and are not prepared to deal with, program evaluation.

In reality, depending on the research design, a program evaluation's involvement of statistics could range from few to plenty. Additionally, program evaluation is not for the wrongfully stereotyped science nerds only. It is a lively and exciting process that many human service providers have the needed expertise to contribute to and enjoy. Royse, Thyer, Padgett, and Logan (2001) state that "program evaluation is a practical endeavor, not an academic exercise, and not an attempt to build theory or necessarily to develop social science knowledge" (p. 2).

Program evaluation employs both quantitative approaches and qualitative approaches. Each approach provides the needed and unique set of data to evaluate the program. Many quantitative approaches employ the deductive ways of evaluating programs; while qualitative approaches use many of the inductive methods. Often, both approaches are used to provide a comprehensive understanding and evaluation of programs.

In writing a grant proposal, the applicant agency is making an argument that it has the understanding of the identified problems and knows how to address the problems. The grant proposal is then the agency's plan of intervention that follows the argument. Moore (1998) defines an argument "as a group of statements, one of which—the conclusion—is claimed to follow the others—the premises" (p. 2). Therefore, an argument "consists of three parts—a group of premises, a conclusion, and an implicit claim" (p. 5). In the case of a program proposal, the group of premises is the basic belief and understanding that support the proposed program. The conclusion is the group of proposed interventions and services. The claim is the expected outcomes. Program evaluation, therefore, is an attempt to assess the proposed argument. Evaluation is the assessment and investigation of whether the conclusions follow the premises and that the claims can be substantiated. Conversely, an evaluation could examine whether premises support conclusions. This concept of "argument" provides the basis for the use of a logic model that is to be discussed in Chapter 3.

Moore (1998) further explains the difference between deductive argument and inductive argument. She cites the classic example of deductive reasoning that "All men are mortal. Socrates is a man. Therefore, Socrates is mortal" (p. 5). From a general truth or premise, a person draws a specific conclusion. The premises, in fact, contain more information than the conclusion, and the conclusion follows from the premises. In this situation, no matter how much more information is available on Socrates, he is still mortal and the conclusion still stands. Deductive reasoning provides a more precise and confident assertion than that from inductive reasoning.

In an inductive argument example, individual specific situations are used to make the generalization "Socrates was mortal. Sappho was mortal. Cleopatra was mortal. Therefore, all people are mortal" (Moore, 1998, p. 6). The premises of three people's situations become the evidence and the basis for the conclusion that applies to all people. The conclusion carries more information than the premises, and could be altered as new information arises and becomes incorporated into the body of knowledge. The inductive conclusion is more of the nature of the probable, correlative, or contributory than that of a more causal determination of deductive reasoning.

Qualitative and quantitative evaluation approaches complement each other, in that they help tell the program "stories" more comprehensively with both structure and contents, with hard data and human touch. Most evaluation efforts employ both approaches at the same time.

Quantitative and Deductive Approaches

Quantitative approaches of evaluation usually involve the application of experimental or quasi-experimental research designs that may include the use of control and experimental groups. This first involves defining the research or evaluation question, and then developing hypotheses. Part of the research interest is the presence and absence of certain interventions or independent variables. The effects of the interventions on certain dependent variables (i.e., results) are objectively evaluated and measured. Often this process involves a larger number of respondents who make up the sample size and the use of validated data collection procedures and instruments.

Program proposal often starts from a particular program philosophy or belief, which is further operationalized into a working hypothesis. Within the context of a program philosophy, the proposal will further derive program goals and objectives and to develop activities. It is expected that these planned activities will bring about the desirable changes that support the program philosophy or belief. Many human service providers believe the behavior of at-risk youths is the result of a lack of significant adults that could provide meaningful relationships and proper guidance. Based on this belief and the working hypothesis (i.e., youth who have a regular association with a positive adult figure are less likely to get involved in high-risk behaviors), the agency organizes a 12-month youth mentoring program (independent variable and intervention), structured through several major objectives.

During this twelve month program period, the agency uses a variety of evaluation strategies, including probability sampling, pre- and postmeasures (preexperimental or experimental designs), and service recording to assess the program's performance. The agency wants to know if and how the mentoring program works. It gathers information and evaluation data from program participants and other relevant information sources.

Deductively, the agency compiles and analyzes data from a large number of the program participants. Through the results of evaluation, the agency develops both general and specific knowledge. It can claim that a data-supported finding, such as the effects of the agency's mentoring program, suggests that such intervention can help bring at-risk youth back to school. If Johnny is an at-risk youth new to the program, the agency can apply the previous evaluation findings and make a confident generalization or assertion that the mentoring program will be helpful for Johnny.

Many variables—including the basic unpredictable nature of human beings and the ethical concerns of manipulation of human variables—make *pure* deductive and quantitative evaluation approaches involving human subjects very difficult and complicated tasks. They require extensive oversight and sufficient resources and funding. Everyday program evaluations, however, do not require the same kind of rigor like many academic or medical researches and evaluations. Logical and well controlled experimental designs are not only feasible for many program evaluation tasks, but also beneficial to program monitoring and improvement.

Qualitative and Inductive Approaches

Royse (1999, p. 278) describes the characteristics of qualitative research. First, it does not involve interventions, experimental designs, or manipulations of variables. Second, it is naturalistic in that it studies subjects in their own natural environment as they grow and change. Similarly, the research question evolves and changes. Third, participant observation provides the in-depth understanding of the identified issues through observations and interviews. Fourth, qualitative research does not require large sample size, and the small sample size could also yield valuable information. Fifth, there is little use of measurement and numeric values. Through the use of his or her eyes and ears, the researcher is the tool of measurement. Sixth, the use of journalistic narrative helps the researchers to have an in-depth and detailed look of a situation. Seventh, much of the qualitative research is exploratory in nature. Finally, the researcher is a learner but not an expert.

Yegidis, Weinbach, Morrison-Rodriguez (1999, p. 127) have similar assertion of qualitative research methods. The qualitative approaches are: (a) subjective, (b) designed to seek understanding rather than explanation, (c) reliant on inductive logic, (d) designed to generate hypotheses, (e) designed to process data as received, and (f) made to use the researcher as the data collection instrument.

Qualitative evaluation provides many qualities that quantitative evaluation is unable to offer. Most importantly, it has the human face in its evaluation findings. Qualitative evaluation employs a variety of theoretical approaches and data collection methods. To name a few, one can find grounded theory approaches, ethnographic studies, case studies, observations, interviews, and focus group. Through these data collection methods, qualitative evaluations look into the relations and dynamics of what happened during the course of the service delivery. They are interested in the subjective reality and personal account of experience. Unlike quantitative approaches, hypotheses are not predetermined. Hypotheses, if any, may arise as a result of the data collected or from the insight developed during the data collection process.

Qualitative evaluation is a more empowering evaluation approach. Populations under study often are involved in the data collection process as collaborators than as subjects of studies. Formative or process information of the program and its participants can provide feedback for the program and the people in a rather timely manner. People are more engaged in the process and more informed about the preliminary results.

Qualitative evaluation is also more suitable to assess variables or situations that are hard to quantify or more subtle issues such as culturally specific behaviors and personal morale. Collecting data in natural settings allows qualitative evaluation to detect subtle and nonconventional behaviors more easily.

Inductive reasoning supports many of the qualitative evaluations. Inductively, people can learn about situations and make generalizations through a variety of patterns. Moore (1998) lists "the argument by analogy, inductive generalization, hypothetical reasoning, and the causal argument" (p. 7). She further explains that learning through analogy involves the use of similar situations to comprehend new or little known situation. Using information from a member of a set to make generalization to all members of that set is an inductive generalization. Hypothetical reasoning uses evidence logically to test against the conclusion in a more "scientific" approach. Causal argument is a special type of hypothetical reasoning that uses evidence to logically establish or against a claim that one event causes another. These patterns of inductive reasoning provide a variety of ways for designing and conducting qualitative evaluation.

Summary

Grant writing is a specific product of the program planning process. This chapter presents a simple program planning formula. There are differences between a grant and a contract; nevertheless, they are both attempts to address particular service needs. Needs assessment is usually the first step of any planning and grant writing efforts. There are both qualitative and quantitative ways to identify, understand, and express the needs that are targeted by the planning and evaluation tasks.

References

Coley, S., & Scheinberg, C. (1990). *Proposal writing.* Newbury Park, CA: Sage.

Lewis, J., Lewis, M., Packard, T., & Souflee, F. (2001). *Management of human service programs* (3rd ed.). Belmont, CA: Brooks/Cole.

Mayer, R. (1985). *Policy and program planning: A developmental perspective.* Englewood Cliffs, NJ: Prentice Hall.

Moore, K. (1998). *Patterns of inductive reasoning.* (4th ed.). Dubuque, IA: Kendall/Hunt Publishing Company.

Royse, D. (1999). *Research methods in social work* (3rd ed.). Belmont, CA: Brooks/Cole.

Royse, D., Thyer, B., Padgett, D., & Logan, T. (2001). *Program evaluation: An introduction* (3rd ed.). Belmont, CA: Brooks/Cole.

Rubin, A., & Babbie, E. (1997). *Research methods for social work* (3rd ed.). Pacific Grove, CA: Brooks/Cole.

Yegudis, B., Weinbach, R., & Morrison-Rodriguez, B. (1999). *Research methods for social workers* (3rd ed.). Boston: Allyn and Bacon.

GRANT PROPOSAL:
A WRITTEN PROGRAM PLAN

Through a step-by-step process with examples, and by following a logic model, this chapter will present a grant writing process that is also a program planning process. The end of the chapter includes a sample proposal review report, to illustrate the fact that there is always room for improvement for any proposals. This grant writing and program planning process will include: defining the purpose and the importance of the program, describing the service environment and needs addressed, identifying target populations, defining measurable and attainable goals and objectives, scheduling activities and time lines, detailing staffing and management issues, developing an appropriate budget, recognizing an agency's capacity, and developing an evaluation plan.

Before we get into the "nuts and bolts" of grant writing, we would like to share with readers two practical observations.

The chance of whether a grant proposal is funded or not rests on 50% quality, 25% luck, and 25% connections. Quality proposal writing will put the proposal ahead of the crowd and make it competitive. However, the political and social status of both the organization and the grant writer, as well as the level of connection to the decision makers, amounts to a considerable portion of the funding determination. The sheer luck or being in the right place at the right time also makes the world of difference. Consequently, new grant writers should not be disappointed when they are not able to land a successful major grant in the first trial. It may need several trials to improve the writing skills, continued development of connections, and luck!

Writing is a passion that comes naturally for some. It is a drag and a cause for anxiety for others. Grant proposal writing requires a different kind of writing skill than that of writing novels. It is, however, learnable and requires practice. Even a good writer encounters writing block, or has trouble parsing what he or she wrote the day before. One of our colleagues, who is a scholar and a fine writer, declares that he routinely needs to write the same sentence seven times before it is to his liking and becomes understandable to others. In grant writing, it is not uncommon for writers to come across writing blocks, to not understand or like what they wrote. Some were surprised to learn that their readers failed to understand the meaning of a paragraph that is perfectly clear to the writers. We have found that it's helpful when you: (a) organize materials, (b) show willingness to revise many times, and (c) keep someone who has no knowledge of your program close at hand to proofread and provide commentary of your draft proposal.

Request for Proposal

Funding agencies usually announce the availability of funding through the issuing of a Request for Proposal (RFP) or Request for Applications (RFA). A notice to the public will generally be distributed and followed by the release and availability of the RFA. Applicant agencies usually have about 6 to 8 weeks to respond to the RFA. The RFA details the major and important information for the proposal application. Usually, it includes all the important dates and due dates. It also highlights the focus of the funding, eligibility of applicants, and what kind of program that it is looking to fund. Some of the federal or major funding foundations will issue a batch of RFAs together as a booklet, while some will only issue individual RFAs. For funding sources that have more rigorous requirements, such as the federal Center for Substance Abuse Prevention or the Robert Wood Johnson Foundation, their RFAs can be quite lengthy and detailed. Some other RFAs for smaller funding are relatively shorter. No matter how long or short the RFA is, the applicant agency should dissect and study the document to gain a fine understanding of the requirements, expectations, and limitations of that particular RFA. Box 3.1 portrays a sample of a condensed RFA announcement.

Logic Model for Program Development

The logic model is a program design approach that emphasizes logical connections between causes or contributing factors to the program objectives, activities, and outcomes. For more than a decade, various federal offices adopted and used the logic model, including the former Office of Substance Abuse Prevention (OSAP), Center for Substance Abuse Prevention (CSAP), and Center for Substance Abuse Treatment (CSAT). The logic model starts off by thoroughly reviewing the literature and identifying causes such as risk and protective factors. Next, the development of specific and measurable program objectives occurs, along with the design of coordinated intervention activities to fulfill the stated objectives. Finally, the model incorporates a detailed and rigorous evaluation component, in order to assess and document process and outcomes of the attainment of the specified objectives (OSAP, 1992).

Using logic model is a rational problem solving approach to program planning. The planning process is, however, not necessarily a linear sequential and rigid one. In an ever-changing environment, factors including the political economy, availability of resources, and timing make a step-by-step straight-line approach impossible and infeasible to map. Program planning process is more of a circular and spiral process; each step will be taken, evaluated, revisited, and refined. The logic model provides a framework to include all the necessary steps for a planning process that leads to the attainment of the desirable program results. Figure 3.1 provides a simple example of a logic model.

Writing a Grant Proposal

A grant proposal for human services is a written presentation of a program plan. This plan details how the applicant will approach the identified needs or problem with their proposed course of actions. Usually, the narrative portion of a grant proposal includes the following major sections:

Abstract
Table of contents
Specific aims/background and significance/needs and problem statement
Target populations
Approaches and methods
Long- and short-term goals
Process, outcome, and impact objectives
Activity plans and scheduling (timeline)
Evaluation plan
Agency capacity and project management
Budget and budget justifications

BOX
3.1 **DHHS GRANT ANNOUNCEMENT #911**

Request for Proposal (RFP)

The Department of Health and Human Services (DHHS) announces the availability of support for new service projects that address the critical needs of the low-income, underserved or at-risk population in the United States. The funding is authorized under Section 123 of the 2002 Public Well-Being Act. A total of ten million dollars ($10,000,000.00) is earmarked for FY2003/2004.

The DHHS is interested in receiving applications for projects that are innovative and well developed in addressing critical needs of the targeted communities. All funded projects should begin no earlier than July 2003 and be completed no later than June 30, 2004. Both local government and private nonprofit human service agencies are eligible to apply for funding support. Applications under this announcement must be received at DHHS Grant Management Office no later than **4:00 p.m. on January 15, 2003.** Absolutely no late applications will be accepted after the deadline.

All applications should include the following sections:

 1. Abstract—*45 lines max.*
 2. Table of Contents—*2 pages max.*
 3. Specific Aims (Needs/Problems, Working Hypothesis, Objectives, Interventions, etc.)—*3 pages max.*
 4. Target Populations—*2 pages max.*
 5. Approaches and Methods (Project Goals and Objectives, Activities, Time Line, etc.)—*6 pages max.*
 6. Evaluation Plan—*3 pages max.*
 7. Agency Capacity and Project Management—*3 pages max.*
 9. Budget and Budget Justification—*3 pages max.*
10. Community Support—*no page limit.*
11. References and Appendices—*no page limit.*

Agencies that are interested in applying for the funding support must submit a **letter of intent** to DHHS **no later than September 30, 2002.** The letter should briefly describe the proposed project, including project goals, target population(s), proposed activities and location(s), and the name of a contact person. Only applicants who have submitted a letter of intent on time will be eligible to apply. Applicants are encouraged to attend the **technical assistance workshop** held in Washington, DC on November 20, 2002 and then in Sacramento, CA on November 22, 2002. Detailed instructions for preparing proposals for this announcement will be given in these technical assistance workshops. DHHS program staff will also be available to answer questions.

For further information, please write or call DHHS.

Abstract

An abstract is a summary of the proposal. About 45 single-spaced lines or one page is usually the recommended length. It is among the first few pages of a big proposal, as well as one of the last things—but not a last-minute task—that a grant writer will prepare before the proposal is sent out to the funding organization. An abstract may be the shortest section of a proposal; it is, however, the most read and most important section of a proposal. It is among the first few pages that the proposal readers would read and form the important first impression. For busy readers or readers who are not main reviewers for your proposal, this may be the only page they use to know your proposal. Their understanding of your proposal from this abstract may be the basis

Logic Model for an Alcohol and Drug Prevention Project for High Risk Youth

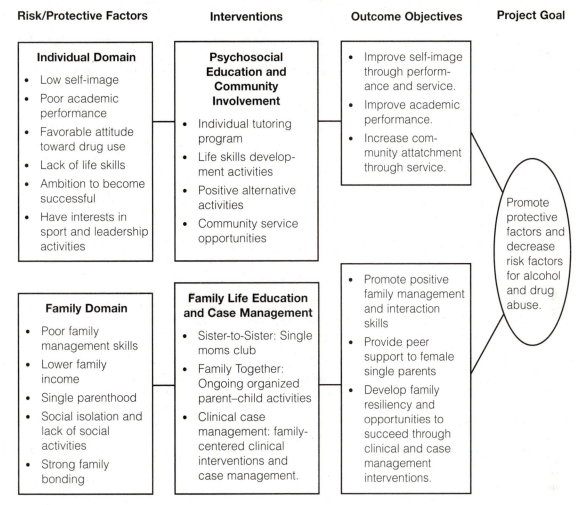

Risk/Protective Factors	Interventions	Outcome Objectives	Project Goal
Individual Domain • Low self-image • Poor academic performance • Favorable attitude toward drug use • Lack of life skills • Ambition to become successful • Have interests in sport and leadership activities	**Psychosocial Education and Community Involvement** • Individual tutoring program • Life skills development activities • Positive alternative activities • Community service opportunities	• Improve self-image through performance and service. • Improve academic performance. • Increase community attachment through service.	Promote protective factors and decrease risk factors for alcohol and drug abuse.
Family Domain • Poor family management skills • Lower family income • Single parenthood • Social isolation and lack of social activities • Strong family bonding	**Family Life Education and Case Management** • Sister-to-Sister: Single moms club • Family Together: Ongoing organized parent–child activities • Clinical case management: family-centered clinical interventions and case management.	• Promote positive family management and interaction skills • Provide peer support to female single parents • Develop family resiliency and opportunities to succeed through clinical and case management interventions.	

FIGURE 3.1 Sample logic model

they use for deciding their ranking of your proposal. It is important to make sure this is well written and that it represents your proposal effectively and succinctly.

An abstract is also used as the project's summary for the various reports of the funding sources, such as the report to the community and to the board of directors. Internally, applicant agencies often use project abstracts for their own reporting and orientation for various constituencies. A proposal abstract (see Box 3.2 for a sample) is a short but important document with multiple functions. Typically, it includes the following information:

Name of agency
Type of organization
Purpose and objectives of the project
Specific interventions for the project
Target population: demographic, age, race, gender, SES, special needs, etc.
Location(s) and setting(s) of project
Relevance of the proposed project to the funding intentions.

BOX
3.2 SAMPLE ABSTRACT

Asian Americans Service Agency (AASA) is a private, nonprofit, community-based organization located in Kingstown, Santa Maria County, California. Since 1976, AASA has been serving the Asian American communities, advocating on behalf of the needs and interests of Santa Maria County's diverse Asian American populations; helping new immigrants and refugees to adjust to a multicultural society and to improve their overall quality of life.

Santa Maria County has the tenth largest Asian refugee population in the United States with 100,000 in 2000. That is an increase of 160% since 1990. The growth is associated with the expansion of several meatpacking plants in the area. Asian Americans make up 15% of the county population and mostly live in east Acetown, according to the 2000 Census. Contrary to the myth of the model minority, Asian Americans in the County, particularly youth, have experienced drastic increases in school drop-outs, emotional and conduct disorders, and delinquency. Substance abuse and gang violence particularly concern the parents, teachers, and local law enforcement agencies of the community. Social services to this population, however, is rather limited.

Consistent with the funding requirements, AASA is proposing the New Generation program, a five-year demonstration project providing culturally competent substance abuse prevention services to high-risk Cambodian, Laotian, and Vietnamese youth and their families. Although many of these youth are American born and live in the contemporary American culture in schools, they also live in their native culture at home. The logic model for the project is based on the working hypothesis that Southeast Asian refugee youth, who do not have positive cultural identities or experiences and have little opportunities for achievement according to their cultural norms, have lower self-image and are at high risk for alcohol and drug abuse and other dysfunctional behaviors.

The New Generation project will provide three areas of services. First, a Youth Cultural Center will be established in east Acetown, providing a focal point for cultural, social, and educational activities for the target population and their families. Second, a school-based program will provide for two Weekend Cultural and Language Schools for Vietnamese and Laotian children, six support groups for the target teens in three local middle schools, and counseling and referral services for the children and their families. Third, to complement the youth center components and to strengthen family relations, the project will organize a Family Ties component. This will involve and empower parents by connecting them with the project as volunteers, instructors, storytellers, advisory board members, and participants with their children. It is expected that this project will serve about 1,500 target youth and their families.

Table of Contents

The table of contents provides the road map for your readers to understand the structure of the applicant proposal and assists them to find the information they want. It should be a clear and uncomplicated list that is simple to use, while detailed enough to refer to the right place for information. During the proposal writing process, the table of contents also serves as a checklist and framework to guide the development of the proposal. After the proposal is done, correct headings and page numbers will then be transferred to the working contents. It is one of the first sections to develop and the last section to complete.

For example, a Center for Substance Abuse Prevention demonstration project, which requires a detailed program plan, an evaluation, and proper government forms and documents, will have a table of contents as displayed in Box 3.3.

Specific Aims

This section presents the rationale and basis for the development, and possibly the approval for funding for this grant proposal. It also provides a brief overview of the proposed project.

BOX
3.3   SAMPLE TABLE OF CONTENTS

1. Application for Federal Assistance (Form 424)
2. Budget: Nonconstruction Program (Form 424A)
   Letter of Intent for Indirect Cost
3. Abstract
4. Table of Contents
5. Narrative
   A. Specific Aims
   B. Specific Outcome Objectives
   C. Target Populations
   D. Approach and Methods
   E. Evaluation Plan
   F. Project Management/Implementation Plan
   G. Project Staff and Organization
   H. Budget Justification and Existing Resources
   I. Confidentiality/Participant Protection

6. Checklist (PHS-5161-1, p. 18)
7. Certifications and Assurances
   A. Assurances: Nonconstruction Programs (Form 424B)
   B. Certification
   C. Civil Right Assurance (45CFR80)
   D. Assurance Concerning the Handicapped (45CFR84)
   E. Assurance Concerning Sex Discrimination (45CFR86)
   F. Assurance Concerning Age Discrimination (45CFR90&91)
   G. Letters from IRS and State Franchise Tax Board

8. Appendices
   Appendix 1:   Resumes/Job Descriptions
   Appendix 2:   Other Support
   Appendix 3:   Letter to/from Single State Agency
   Appendix 4:   Letters of Commitment from Collaborating Organizations/Individuals
   Appendix 5:   Statement of Commitment to National/Cross-Site Evaluation
   Appendix 6:   Organizational and Project Structures
   Appendix 7:   Certification Concerning Supplantation of Funds
   Appendix 8:   Data Collection Instruments and Scales: Violence Index . . .
   Appendix 9:   Sample Consent Forms
   Appendix 10:   Activities Gantt Chart
   Appendix 11:   References
   Appendix 12:   Board of Directors List
   Appendix 13:   Curricular Outlines: ATOD Prevention Class, Feel Good Program . . .
   Appendix 14:   Letters of Support

Different funding announcements refer to this section with different names: needs and problem statement, the background and significance, or the literature review. In fact, this section often includes all of the aforementioned elements as subsections.

The main concern here is to present the case that you, the applicant agency, know what you are doing and why you are doing what you are proposing to do. It will also show your proposed interventions are guided by sound theoretical models and supported by all concerned constituencies. The applicant agency knows the theoretical models well, receives input from clients and community, and has developed a set of coordinated programs both theoretically sound and operationally feasible.

This section is like saying: "This is the current condition: We understand the dynamics of the situation in our target areas and how they affect our target populations. Based on the objective information, professional knowledge, practice experience, and support from the affected population, we propose the following promising interventions." The writing of this section, like the rest of the proposal, has to be logical and succinct. Since detailed information on intervention is provided later on in the approaches and methods section, you only need a summary or preview of program objectives and interventions in this section.

Needs/Problem Statement

Many agencies spend tremendous amounts of time writing up the case justifying an urgent situation or problem that needs to be addressed. Meanwhile they are minimal in writing how they are going to address the problems they identified. Most of the time, the funding agency has a fairly good idea of the identified problem. Otherwise they would not allocate funding to support service projects that address the problem. If the funding source is already well aware of the situation, the applicant agencies may not need to spend too much time "preaching to the choir." They should use this section to highlight the uniqueness of their situation, their unique insight of the situation, and their innovative approaches that address the problem. Instead of telling the funding source excessively where the agency is coming from (the known needs and problems), the agency may want to tell the funding source where it is going (objectives, interventions, and outcomes).

Coley and Scheinberg (1990) provide a useful outline for the write-up of a needs/problem statement: "The needs/problem statement examines what is happening that requires attention, attempts to explain why it is happening, and discusses what currently is being done to address it" (p. 40). The conceptual framework for development of a needs/problem statement (see Box 3.4 as well) can be described as:

> Clients with "A" characteristics and background live in "B" conditions/environments and have "C" problems/needs that are caused by "D". Clients are blocked from solving these problems because of "E". This problem is related to other problems "F" and [have] "G" short- and long-term impact if not addressed. The impact of their needs/problems on the community is "H." Others have addressed their needs/problems by doing "I"; the results of their interventions have been "J." The most promising strategy for interventions is "K" (p. 41).

In this example, "A," "B," "C," and "D" are the characteristics, risk/protective factors, and presenting problems. The "E," "F," "G," and "H" are barriers, causes, consequences, and the working hypothesis. The "I" and "J" are the successful experience. This conceptual framework also forms the basic working hypothesis for the project and its interventions "K."

Coley and Scheinberg (1990) assert that the applicant should attempt to show he or she has a complete understanding, and the best intervention model, of the problem that the funder seeks to address. Based on the guideline proposed by Coley and Scheinberg, Box 3.5 on page 26 shows a simplified outline for the write up of the needs and problem statement.

The needs/problem statement frames the working hypothesis that is the general belief that guides the development of a project proposal. This belief could be based on the applicants' theoretical orientation, philosophical position, practice experience, agency mission, and other assumptions. It is not a research hypothesis, waiting to be validated. It is, however, a hunch or an educated speculation of what could be done to address the identified needs or problems. For example, most mentoring programs for at-risk children believe that positive role modeling and guidance from mature individuals (mentors) who care and maintain constant and purposive

| BOX 3.4 | SAMPLE NEEDS AND PROBLEM STATEMENT |

The 650 students aged 12 to 15, who come from mostly low-income families in the inner city of Springfield, are attending the neighborhood ABC middle school. They have a 50% dropout rate associated with poor academic performances and behavioral problems. Their last year statewide standardized math and reading test scores ranked at the bottom of the thirtieth percentile. Substance abuse, gang violence, and truancy are frequent problems that draw serious concerns from parents, school authorities, law enforcement agencies, and child welfare professionals.

A systematic survey of teachers, parents, and the targeted students last semester reveals that many of these students are academically underprepared. Many suggest that a one-to-one tutoring program, along with enrichment activities during after-school hours that involves parents, is an effective approach to address the problem. Currently no such service is available to these students either in school or in the community.

The continuation of students failing from school is believed to have high correlations to the increase of gang activities in the communities. These situations have brought about the high crime rate in the community and an increased number of youth not prepared for gainful employments. Recently, the only grocery store and the only bank in the community have decided to close down their operations in this community. The long-term economic, educational, and human impacts of these situations not only affect the target community but also the surrounding neighborhoods.

The local police and PTA have tried to bring in the DARE program to address the substance abuse problems. The Boys and Girls Club has also started a small after-school recreation program. These programs have gained positive feedback from parents and teachers; however, due to transportation and staffing issues, only 30 students have been able to participate in these programs annually.

The applicant, ABC agency, is proposing a comprehensive intervention program titled Kids Success . . .

---

contacts with their assigned children (mentees) will bring about desirable changes and benefits to the children.

While writing the needs/problem statement, one should avoid the mistakes of circular reasoning or tautology. Circular reasoning is like a dog chasing its own tail: it will go round and round in a circle. For example, one may argue the reason for having the proposed senior community center is because there is none in the target community. Conversely, one may also argue that since there is not a senior center in the community, therefore it should develop one. The argument has no end and no beginning. The best way to spot and to get out of a circular reasoning is to accept that the argument of "lacking what's proposed" is not a good argument. Start thinking about exactly why the community needs the proposed intervention. Without a senior center, what would happen to the older adult population in the community? What can be accomplished in the senior center, if it were established? A strong statement focuses on why the intervention is needed, and what would happen if the implementation of the intervention goes through or not—but not on the intervention itself. The intervention is proposed to meet clients' or community needs; it is not proposed for its own existence.

In addressing the issues of barriers to service, particularly those related to cultural competency, a proposal writer may wish to look into the five As: accessibility, availability, awareness, appropriateness, and acculturation. The applicant agency should assess these five areas as

BOX
3.5   SIMPLIFIED OUTLINE FOR WRITE-UP OF NEEDS AND PROBLEM STATEMENT

Each year, (# of people) experience or are affected by (the problem). The situation has (gotten better, worse, or unchanged) over the (period of time). According to (professional and academic based objective data, and the subjective but compassionate data), (the identified contributing and causal factors) are the main reasons for the current conditions in the target area and/or of the target populations. These factors are (similar to or different from) the (national, state, or regional data). The consequences for not addressing the problem are _____. The benefits of taking appropriate actions to address the problem are _____. There have been some successful and effective intervention strategies. They include _____. Given the unique local situation, demands, and barriers, the most promising interventions are _____.

they relate to the proposed services. It is particularly important when the proposed services target a cultural or ethnic population. Cultural factors become both the barriers and the facilitators. The degree of acculturation of service recipients plays a vital role in the design of the services.

According to Yuen (1999), "accessibility refers to both geographical and cultural relevance as well as difficulties in service delivery. . . . Availability refers to the existence, recruitment, and retention of service, clients, and qualified service provider" (p. 109). Awareness refers to the target population's knowledge about the identified issues and the available services. Appropriateness is about suitability and acceptability of the services that are developmentally and culturally competent. Finally, "[a]cculturation refers to the quality and extent of expose to the dominant American culture and the degree of functioning within the dominant culture" (p. 110). Ideally, culturally competent service programs are available to meet the identified needs in an appropriate manner. Target populations are aware of the service, and they can geographically and culturally access the services.

Coley and Scheinberg (1990) suggest some strategies that applicants can use to strengthen their rationales to support their proposed program:

Clearly identifies the target group
Meets a client/community needs
Is cost effective
Is a novel approach
Builds upon the work of others
Uses existing resources
Promotes interagency cooperation
Fits with the funder's mandate/mission
Has the potential of being replicated (p. 48)

Literature Review

The review of literature provides objective support data and rationales for the arguments in the proposal and the development of the interventions. It covers both professional, academic, as well as documentary materials. It reports both the historical account of the identified needs or problems, as well as the most current thinking on the issue. This is not a collection of cut-and-pasted information from unverified sources or personal beliefs. It is a well-developed review of relevant information from creditable sources to lean support to the approaches presented in the proposal. It helps establish and explain the theoretical foundation of the development of the proposal and its interventions. It should not be a "social problem" paper that explores the various aspects of an identified problem or provides a laundry list of needs and problems. It is a write-up that helps readers to have a better understanding and appreciation of the identified problems. It also validates the appropriateness and the quality of the proposal.

Box 3.6 provides a framework that a program planner or grant writer can use to develop the Specific Aims section of the proposal. The client systems can be the multiple target populations that the proposed intervention will affect. They may be the students who are substance abusers, their parents, their schools, and neighborhoods. The identified needs and problems for each of the target population should then be discussed with support data from professional literature, creditable reports from various sources, and experience from the very people who are affected. Based on this information, proper objectives will be developed with detailed intervention activities. The reasons and the appropriateness for the choices of intervention activities should also be considered. These reasons may include cultural, developmental, social, and other factors that make the interventions appropriate and effective in achieve the intended outcomes. Box 3.7 on page 29 provides an example of the specific Aim information.

Target Populations

The applicant needs to make a case here that the target population is especially at risk or in an urgent situation and needs to be served. Briefly, justify why this particular group and not the other groups who may be equally in need of services should be funded; for example, timing, recent successful experience, or recommendations according to local private and government reports. Write more than just plain statistical descriptions. Cite creditable sources of information to support the claims. Box 3.8 is a sample outline for describing target populations.

Approaches and Methods

Many years ago, in a hamburger chain commercial, an older lady asked a famous question: "Where's the beef?" In proposal writing, approaches and methods section is the "beef" for the proposal. This section will lay out the proposed interventions or solutions that are intending to bring about changes on issues identified in the previous sections. Some funding sources refer to this section as goals and objectives, and activities and timelines.

Since this section can be rather extensive and detailed, it is a good idea to start it off with an introduction or summary of the proposed project goals and plan. To reiterate the appropriateness and the feasibility of the proposed intervention and activities, the applicant may wish to discuss its abilities to gain support and access to the target population. A well-designed intervention program is worthless if it fails to reach the intended population.

From Vision to Mission, Goals, Objectives, and Activities
Vision, mission, purpose, direction, goals, objectives, activities, and tasks are terms that proposal writers and program planners use. They are also terms that confuse the users and readers alike. Each organization, or its program, has an ultimate ideal state that it wishes to achieve. It is like the beautiful view that rests beyond the horizon, or a pot of gold at the end of the rainbow. This view or "vision" is rather far away and out-of-reach, but is a fascinating and desirable state. When you put this

BOX 3.6	SPECIFIC AIMS DEVELOPMENT FRAMEWORK

Client systems	Needs or problems	Information sources: literature, key informants, etc.	Objectives	Interventions and activities	Why these interventions?
A					
B					
C					

BOX 3.7	SAMPLE OUTLINE FOR WRITING SPECIFIC AIMS

1. Statement of Problems / Issues to be addressed by the project

- Identify only those problem areas, needs, risk/protective factors, or behavioral and social indicators that will be addressed by the project's interventions. There may be many important factors that are related to the identified problems and needs. However, the proposed project may not and should not be a for-all and cure-all program. It has a limited scope, focus, and boundary.

- Indicate processes used to select these factors, such as (a) clients and community's input, (b) literature, and (c) agency experience.

2. Working Hypothesis for the project

- Each program carries a particular belief or philosophy that motivates and guides the development of the program. This belief or hunch is the program philosophy that can be a statement in the form of a working hypothesis.

- e.g., Young students who attend supervised recreational activities after school are less likely to become school dropouts.

- e.g., Supervised after-school recreational activities will increase the target students' likelihood of doing well in school and staying in school.

3. Briefly describe the expected outcomes, and interventions proposed to achieve these outcomes

- Briefly indicate the (a) outcome objectives and (b) intervention strategies used to address the problems/needs with a particular client system.

- e.g., To improve the parenting skills of teen fathers through an 8-week peer-training program in school.

- Describe the theoretical basis, process, and rationale for selecting these interventions.

- Discuss the effectiveness and relevance of interventions: (a) applicant's experience, (b) relevant literature, and (c) community input.

**BOX
3.8**   **SAMPLE OUTLINE FOR WRITING TARGET POPULATIONS**

---

1. **Describe the target environment such as the community, neighborhood, city, district, etc.**

   Describe the socioeconomic status (SES), race and ethnicity distribution, and other urban/rural/suburban classification of the target environment.

2. **Describe the population(s) to be served**

   Provide and describe the basic demographic data about the target population, such as race/ethnicity, age, gender, urban/rural/suburban, and SES.

3. **Whether members of particular groups that have recognized great needs**

   Discuss whether the target population are from special high-risk groups such as latchkey children, abused youth, court referrals, homeless families, victims of violence, individuals with physical or mental disabilities, low-income families, and other disadvantaged groups.

4. **Who and how many will participate or be served**

   Discuss the types and number of target clients, family members, and service providers involved. Who and how many will be served each year? How many will be served during the whole project period? Who and how many will be served in each of the proposed intervention or activity?

---

vision into words, it becomes a mission statement. An agency's mission statement describes the reasons and the framework for the being of the agency and what the agency is intending to achieve. "Mission statements are relatively permanent expressions of the reason for existence of an organization, and they are not expected to change unless the fundamental reason for existence of the organization changes" (Netting, Kettner, & McMurtry, 1993, p. 174).

A vision or a mission statement, however, is a rather abstract and distant concept. To bring this mission into a more manageable level, an agency will derive from the mission statement a list of major "goals" that are appropriate at that time for the agency. Goals are long-term destinations that are general. They are not necessarily measurable or achievable in the short run. They help limit the scope, however, and operationalize the abstract mission statement. Netting and associates (1993) describe goals as "general statements of expected outcome" (p. 240), "statement(s) of hopes or expectations" (p. 242). They are generally brief , e.g., to improve clients' quality of life.

As goals are not yet concrete and measurable, "objectives" are comparatively short term, measurable, and achievable. Objectives set the parameter and the mechanism of how and what interventions are to be provided. "Objectives spell out the details for each goal in measurable terms, including expected outcomes and the processes to achieve them" (Netting, et al., 1993, p. 240). Objective is defined as a statement of measurable and directional change for a specific population in a specific time period. Gabor, Unrau, and Grinnell (1998) further assert that in addition to being specific, measurable, and directional, an objective has to be meaningful. "A program objective is meaningful when it bears a sensible relationship to the longer-term result to be achieved—the program goal" (p. 88). There has to be a logical and meaningful linkage between program goals and objectives.

Basically, there are three major types of objectives: process, outcome, and impact. Netting and associates (1993) characterize outcome objective as that "specifies the results or outcome to be achieved" and then the process objective "specifies the process to be followed in order to achieve the result" (p. 242). Process objectives describe what activities are to be carried out to achieve the planned result. It answers the questions "Did we do what we set out to do?" and "What happens?" Outcome objectives focus the result of the interventions. For program evaluation, it answers the question of "How well did we do?" Impact objectives are the most abstract and difficult objectives. They identify the collective and accumulative results of the intervention. Impact objectives aim to answer the question of "So what?" Objective is linkage between the program mission and goals and its activities and task. Each goal can have several objectives and, conversely, each objective can have several activities and their associated tasks.

Objectives can be formulated and stated as process, outcome, and impact objectives. In many situations, an objective statement can include both process and outcome (e.g., "To provide 100 units of case management service to at least 20 welfare to work clients resulting in half of the them steadily employed in part-time or full-time positions at the end of the program year.")

For programs that have many objectives, it is a good idea to have a good mix of process and outcome objectives. Certain programs may also require impact objectives. More detailed discussions on varies types of objectives are included in the Evaluation section later in this chapter.

"Activities are lists of tasks that must be undertaken and completed in order to achieve each objective. . . . Activities specify precisely what to be done, by whom, and within what time frame" (Netting, et al., 1993, p. 240). Activities are the implementation and delivery of the actual intervention actions. Activities actualize the objectives and often are the only thing recognized by service recipients. As many activities lead to objectives, which in turn link to the goals and mission, they form a shape similar to that of a triangle. All activities, objectives, and goals point together toward the mission statement on the top of the triangle. This orientation toward the mission statement forms the "direction" or "purpose" of the organization. Figure 3.2 displays these linkages and relationships.

Box 3.9 and 3.10 beginning on page 32 provide two frameworks for writing the approaches and methods section, and one tool to help write better objectives, respectively. The first sample outline lists the basic components for this section. The second and more detailed example includes several objectives and their associated activities. In this example, main objectives are further broken down and organized into subobjectives. A numbering system is used to identify the linkages among objectives and activities.

As the program is writing its program objectives, it is also preparing for the evaluation strategies that go with each of the objectives. There are many ways to develop an evaluation plan. The following Objective and Evaluation Plan Development Form (see Box 3.11 on page 35) provides an example of using a structure to write objective as well as plan to evaluate the objective. This form is based on a worksheet used by Project STAR of Aguirre International, a technical assistance project for AmeriCorps Project of the Corporation for National Service. Program staff can use this form to refine each objective and develop its associated evaluation plan. By completing this form for each objective and attach each objective's data collection instruments for its evaluation strategies, program staff will have an organized operating evaluation manual.

Evaluation Plan

Program evaluation is a type of evaluation research that systematically assesses the achievement of a specific program (Barker, 1999). It is an effort for practical purposes. It is not intended to generate scientific knowledge for theory building or academic accomplishments (Royse, Thyer, Padgett, & Logan, 2001). Program evaluation as an ongoing process is an integral part of the program and is detailed in the form of an evaluation plan.

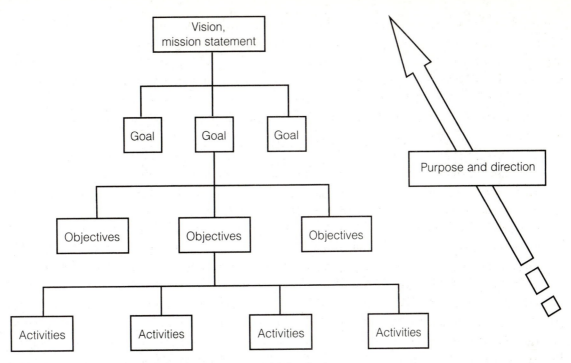

FIGURE 3.2 Linkages and relationships of goals and objectives

An evaluation plan is like a design or a map that the program staffs and evaluators will follow to assess the progress and results of the program. It employs many of the basic social research methodologies, designs, and statistics, driven by the goals and objectives of the program that it intends to evaluate. Therefore, an evaluation plan should be developed, along with the formulation of program goals, objectivities, and activities at the beginning of the program. It is not a last-minute write-up or an afterthought at the end of the program year when reports are due. It is an ongoing process that is an integral part of the program.

Program managers should become knowledgeable about the evaluation process and the utilization of findings from program evaluation. Some human service agencies have internal program evaluators to assess the results of their programs. Certain program situations, however, may call for the use of outside evaluators. When the program managers are not familiar with the work of evaluation or fail to develop the working relations with the evaluators, the benefits of the cooperation between the program and the evaluation will not be maximized. In some situations, when the evaluators are academically more educated and have strong opinions, the evaluation tasks may end up driving the program. Consequently, program activities are done first to produce results for evaluation, but not to serve the clients that it intends to serve. It then is a case of "goal displacement."

Program evaluation for a project intends to achieve three basic objectives and produce three basic types of data:

1. Documentation of program implementation strategies, intervention models, and other process information (process data)
2. Measurement of program outcomes and results (outcome data)
3. Assessment of overall impact and success of the program (impact data).

SAMPLE OUTLINE FOR WRITING APPROACHES AND METHODS SECTION

1. **Introduction/Summary and Goals**
   - What do you try to achieve (goal), and why are your approaches so unique and appropriate?
   - *e.g., The proposed new project aims to reduce violence and substance abuse related problems, and to promote positive functioning of families through educational, social, and recreational prevention and intervention activities, which are specific to the culture, gender, and age of the tar get population.*
   - Present a simplified implementation plan or summary that includes: who (target population), whom (staff), what (programs/activities), where (sites/settings), when (time line) and how (intensity and frequency).

2. **Recruitment, Retention, and Community Support**
   - Detail procedures for identifying, gaining access to, recruiting, retaining, and following up the target groups, as well as other related people and organizations.
   - Discuss anticipated problems for recruitment and retention of clients.
   - Develop plans for culturally and developmentally appropriate interventions.
   - If multiple sites are used, describe and justify.
   - Present plans for coordination with other related programs in the organization and in the community. Indicate evidence of commitment or support from these organizations and individuals.

3. **Objectives and Activities**
   - Objective is defined as a measurable and directional change for a specific population in a specific time period.
   - *e.g., To achieve a 10% (measurable) increase (directional) in grade averages (measurable) for targeted youth (specific population) after (specific time) their completion of the 6-month Dare To Study tutoring program (the intervention).*
   - Interventions/Activities need to be (a) related to the project theoretical mode, (b) fulfill specified objectives, and (c) developmentally and culturally appropriate.

4. **Time Line**
   - Expected schedule for activities by each component. In addition to general narrative description, attach a graphic presentation such as Gantt Chart as an appendix to show activity schedules under each objectivity.
   - Time line also helps grant writer to realize the program's time limitations and the need to plan well for the distribution and implementation of program activities.

Process data documents what happened for the program. They concern the question: "Did the program do what it set out to do?" Outcome data report the extent of which the program achieves or fail to achieve the intended to unintended results. They concern the question: "How well did the program do?" Impact data judge the long-term and sometime transcendental or philosophical consequences of the program. They concern the question: "So what?" Process objectives generate process data for evaluation. It is the same for outcome objectives to provide outcome data and impact objectives gather impact data.

To further illustrate these three types of objectives and data, consider Susan who grew tired and frustrated about her job as a child welfare social worker. She decided to take a weeklong getaway trip to the mountain, staying in a monastery. It was not a party and fun type pleasure trip; instead, it was more or less a personal retreat. Susan wanted to be in peaceful and serene environments to reflect and to think about life in general. She brought along a camera and a

BOX
3.10 **DETAILED SAMPLE GOALS, OBJECTIVES, AND ACTIVITIES**

Project Goal:

The goal of the Can Do project is to prevent the use and abuse of alcohol, tobacco, and other drugs (ATOD)—and associated violence—among high-risk children and adolescents from low-income families in the Sunny City, by reducing associated high-risk factors and promoting positive protective factors. There are three main components of the project: 1. Youth Center, 2. School, and 3. Family.

Component 1—Youth Center

Objective 1

Provide ATOD intervention services to 400 adolescents through the Community Youth Center. Or:

In comparison to the adolescents of the control group in the same school, 25% more of the adolescents who regularly participate in Community Youth Center activities will have a negative attitude toward ATOD use (or will improve school performance by 10%, report a significant increase in their self-image, etc.). Or:

Develop a new community youth center (CYC) service in the Southside of the Sunny City to provide ATOD intervention services to 400 target children and adolescents annually to reduce risk factors that contribute to substance abuse and gang violence.

Objective 1.1

Develop year-round social, recreation, and educational alternative activities after school hours (3:00 PM to 6:00 PM) in CYC for 150 target children, adolescents, and their families beginning month 3 to promote protective factors.

> **Activities:**
>
> **1.1.1** Organize one 15 boys soccer team and one 15 girls soccer team, recruit 10 parents and college youth as coaches, get sponsorship from local business, participate in at least one local tournament.
>
> **1.1.2** Organize 4 interest classes (skateboarding, arts and craft, music, and gardening) for 40 boys and girls. Each class will have 10–15 members and meet weekly for 2 hours on either Wednesday or Friday afternoon.
>
> **1.1.3** Organize a homework-tutoring program for 50 boys and girls. Eight (8) volunteer-tutors will staff the program. It operates daily during school year from 3–6 P.M. at the study hall.

Objective 1. 2

Develop the community support network (community leaders, business, schools, and government) that includes at least 10 target organizations to provide support and advice to the project.

> **Activities:**
>
> **1.2.1** Develop the project Advisory Board within the first 8 months of the project. The Board will meet bi-monthly and should have 6–8 members, including: parents, school representatives, law enforcement officials, and other community members.
>
> **1.2.2** A memorandum of agreement (MOU) will be developed between Ozark Health Awareness Council (OHAC), the Noo Mooney School Board, the XYZ agency, and other participating organizations to formalize the cooperative relationship.

Objective 1.3

Establish the CYC within the first 2 months of the project in the neighborhood of the target population to serve as the base for activities and gathering.

> **Activities:**
>
> **1.3.1** Locate the facility, complete lease agreement and tenant improvement by the end of the first month.
>
> **1.3.2** Recruit Advisory Board members to assist the development of the program.
>
> **1.3.3** Recruit project staff; project director by the beginning of the project, administrative assistant and project coordinators by the second month, other project staff by the third month.

(continued)

BOX
3.10   DETAILED SAMPLE GOALS, OBJECTIVES, AND ACTIVITIES (*CONTINUED*)

Component 2—School

Objective 2

Implement a school based ATOD prevention curriculum (Careful Steps) (curriculum included as attachment) for 100 5th and 6th graders in two primary schools (Powell Rangers School and Pokemount School) of the Noo Mooney School District to facilitate the healthy development of their positive self-identity and social skills. Pre- and posttests with SSDI (the Self-Identity and Social Development Index, designed specifically for this project) and the State Children Self-Assessment Scale (SCAS) will measure the effectiveness of the program and childrenís development in the areas of self-identity and social skills.

Objective 2.1

Revised the "Careful Steps" curriculum within the first 6 month of the project to make it more culturally appropriate to the local population, shortening it from a 24-week curriculum to a 12-week curriculum.

> **Activities:**
>
> **2.1.1** Address copyright issues and secure proper approval from authors.
>
> **2.1.2** Revise the curriculum by the project evaluator and director, to be completed by the end of the fourth month.

Objective 2.2

Implement the curriculum to 100 5th and 6th graders in two partner schools to significantly improve their self-identity and social skills.

> **Activities:**
>
> **2.2.1** Organize students who are referred to the program by teachers into groups of 10 to 15 students from the same grade in the same school. Annually, a total of 8 groups will be organized to meet weekly for 2 hours for 12 weeks during after-school hours.
>
> **2.2.2** Conduct baseline assessment using the SSDI and the SCAS upon referral and then outcome assessment at 3 months after the completion of the training.

Component 3—Family

Objective 3

Promote family functioning through the provision of outreach/home-based family intervention services to 100 high-risk children in two partner schools and their family members/parents annually, in the areas of substance abuse, family violence, mental health, and economic well-being.

Objective 3.1

Provide home-based case management and counseling to 75 families during the first year. Upon referral by teachers and identification of student with behavioral or emotional concerns, project social worker will contact and visit the family. Short-term counseling and case management services will be the main intervention modalities. To assess the quality and effectiveness of this service, 25% of all cases will be evaluated using single subject designs to evaluate clients' progress.

> **Activities:**
>
> **3.1.1** Identify and recruit 75 target families through referrals by teachers, school based groups, and other human service providers, as well as clients' self-referrals.
>
> **3.1.2** Provide 400 hourly family intervention services, such as home visits, counseling, and case management during the first project year.

Objective 3.2

Increase 50 target families' stress management and parenting skills through four 6-week Parents as Teachers training sessions, along with follow up activities, resulting in 60% or 30 families reporting an increase in family coping and family functioning capacities on the Training Evaluation Form.

> **Activities:**
>
> **3.2.1** Implement the four Parents as Teacher trainings by two project social workers in two community facilities closer to the homes of the target families. Each training will include parents or caregivers from up to 14 families. Each training group will have the option of continuing as a parent support group after the six weeks of training is completed.
>
> **3.2.2** Advertise the training and recruit sufficient support from the appropriate partner agencies, such as county child welfare department, social service department, and other private human service providers in the service areas.

BOX
3.11   OBJECTIVE AND EVALUATION PLAN DEVELOPMENT FORM

Program Name:

Objective Title: **Date:**

Activity   Activity
Start Date: **End Date:**   **Staff by:**

Needs Statement:

1. **Activity** Describe the service activity or the delivery structure that you will be providing and evaluating. (Describe the who, what, when, and where that you use to make your outcomes happen.)	
2. **Beneficiaries** Briefly describe the target groups (and the estimated number) your activity will serve.	
3. **Desired Accomplishments and Results** Describe service data or activities (process) that are to be accomplished. Explain what change (outcome) will occur because of the described activity or intervention.	
4. **Indicators** Describe the concrete, observable things you will look at to see whether you are making progress toward your desired result.	
5. **Method/Title of Measure** Describe the method and the instruments or tools you will use to determine if the described change occurs. (e.g., Teacher Opinion Survey)	
6. **Standard of Success** Define a level of success you hope to achieve.	
7. **Respondents and Measurements Schedule** Describe who will complete each instrument and frequency of measures to be taken.	
8. **Data Collection, Aggregation, and Analysis** Describe who will be collecting, aggregating, and analyzing the data and how often.	
9. **Reporting and Dates** Describe who will write the report and how often the report is due.	

Objective Statement: *Example: Volunteer tutors will provide one-on-one tutoring to 50 4th*
Combine 1–6 into a single   *grade students, weekly for 60 minutes for 4 months, resulting in 75% of*
statement of objective.   *those who participate regularly demonstrating improved reading ability,*
as measured by a diagnostic reading test administered prior to and
following the program.

Source: Created by Project STAR. Used with permission of Aguirre International.

notepad to record her journey and to write down her thoughts and feelings. A couple of days after her return, she was having lunch with her friends and showing them some of the photos that she took while she was on that trip, along with some souvenirs. Each of these photos provided a snapshot of her trip. Together, they became a record of this journey. Although the photos were beautiful and interesting, her friends were curious about her assessments of this trip. Her friends asked, "How did you like that trip?", "Did you get what you expected? How did you do that?", and "How was it?" Susan replied, "Very well, I had a wonderful time, I liked it a lot." After lunch, she went back to her little office and sat in her almost broken office chair in front of a big stack of case files. She looked around, took a deep breath, and said to herself, "I am glad that I took that trip. I was able to do most of the things that I planned to do. It was a rather fun and enjoyable time-off from my hectic work and social life. Most importantly, the whole experience provided me an opportunity to reflect and to refresh. Now I am reenergized and have an renewed perspective toward my work and myself."

Susan's photos, souvenirs, and journey log represent the process data that she has to show and to record what she had done or what happen to her during that trip. But the physical evidence didn't tell much about the outcomes or the extent of Susan's satisfaction of the trip. Upon being questioned by her friends, Susan responded on the outcomes of how much she enjoyed the trip and to what extent she was able to have time for herself. Susan was able to satisfactorily achieve what she set out to accomplish. For Susan, a reflective person, this excursion represented more than a pleasant trip to the mountain. It produced an impact that brought her renewed perspectives toward herself and her work.

The intended results of the process evaluation task are to: (a) provide accurate description of the project's development, (b) provide accurate quantitative data on interventions, and (c) prepare qualitative analyses of program activities. Whereas outcome evaluation tasks assess whether certain proposed interventions in fact have effects on the issues addressed by the project, such as the reduction of risk factors; the promotion of protective functioning, increase of leadership skills, development of self-identity, and so on.

The formats of evaluation plans (as shown in Box 3.11) vary according to the program that they intend to evaluate. However, they are likely to include the following components:

1. Process evaluation plan
2. Outcome and impact evaluation plan
3. Data collection and data analysis plan
4. Confidentiality and other ethical considerations
5. Data collection instruments
6. Implications and reporting plan, and others

Program evaluations often are objective-driven. The process and outcome evaluation plans could be developed and organized per each program individual objective. (Detailed discussions of program evaluation and examples are presented in the following chapters of this book.)

Agency Capacity and Project Management

The creditability of the agency is like the creditability of an individual. It is associated with how much confidence and trust others may have in the individual or the organization. The funding applicant needs to convince the funding sources that it is uniquely qualified and competent, and that they can entrust it with the funding and the attainment of the desirable program results. The agency is to show that it has the track records as well as the abilities to design and to carry out the proposed project, if funded. These track records include both the agency's program capacities and the fiscal abilities. Funding source and monitoring entities need to know how the agency plans to manage the project.

One can learn about the agency capacity through reviewing the agency's mission statement, history, structure, programs, accomplishments, and other qualitative and quantitative information. With the increasing emphasis on collaboration and coordination, as well as the concerns over recruitment and retention of clients, agency often needs to show its capacities in community mobilization and connections. One way to show this capacity is to include support letters from relevant organizations and individuals. These may include relevant politicians, partner organizations, and clients or target population.

Management plan details the staffing and their responsibilities, the chain of command, and the project's relations to the other programs within the organization. This management plan reflects the efforts that the agency is willing to commit, the qualifications of the staff, and the division of labors and the cooperation. Box 3.12 provides a sample outline for preparing the agency capacity and project management section. Resumes of current and proposed staff should also be included for review. Detailed job descriptions of each of the positions will help clarify the agency's expectations of the project staff. Box 3.13 gives two examples of such job descriptions.

Budget and Budget Justifications

Budget has always been a great concern for many human service programs. Agencies turn to many types of fund-raising activities, ranging from major grants and contracts to small-scale bake sales to raise money for program expenses and agency operating costs. With the increased demand for accountability and the need to monitor how agencies spend their public money and donations, there is a greater need for a program to have a well-developed budget.

A budget is a financial plan that estimates the costs for implementing a program and the allocation of these costs. There are many formats of budget for programs. The line-item budget is a commonly used model. It details how money will be spent annually for items or categories such as personnel, equipment, and supplies.

Not only should funding applicants detail the dollar amounts for each of the categories, they should also be asked to justify the amount and the allocations. Some agencies prefer to list the budget and detail the justifications on separated pages. Others, however, incorporate the justifications into the budget layout.

The line-item budgetary model has several common categories. Personnel is the cost for hiring or salary for permanent staff. It is often a large expense item on the budget. Generally speaking, a program should not have a personnel cost that exceed 65% of the total budget (i.e., $65,000 for a $100,000 grant).

Salary is not the only cost for having a permanent staff. Each of the position carries a cost for paying the benefits for the employees. These include payroll tax, unemployment benefits, and other health and life insurance costs. Although it varies from agency to agency, generally it means approximately 20% of the employee's salary cost (i.e., 20% of $65,000 is $13,000). The executive director, the fiscal director, the administrative director, the young man who answers the phone, and the nice lady who cleans the office are all part of the operations that make the program possible. They, too, have to be paid. And the cost is the so-called indirect cost. The calculations of indirect cost are again different from agency to agency, and from funding source to funding source. Some funding sources figure the costs in as part of the total project cost; some, however, treat it as a cost that is above and beyond the project cost.

BOX
3.12   SAMPLE OUTLINE FOR AGENCY CAPACITY AND PROJECT MANAGEMENT

---

1. Organizational Structure

- **Agency description:** What it is and what does it do—list of current programs, how does the proposed project complement other current programs and strengthen the whole service delivery net work of the agency.

- *e.g., Open Health Awareness Council (OHAC) is a private, nonprofit, human service agency. It was established in 1975. The agency's current annual budget is $900,000.00. It provides an array of health and human services to 3,000 clients annually. Current programs include the following . . .*

- **Board of Directors:** Describe the structure and functions of the Board. Attach a board members list and structure in appendix section.

- Description of the **organizational structure.** Attach an organizational chart that shows lines of authority and where the proposed project will fit into the organization.

2. Organization Capacity

- Provide evidence that the organization can implement the proposed project.

- Document experience in similar or relevant activities.

- Highlight the agency's abilities to access to the target populations.

- Display expertise in delivering service in the area or in the target community.

- Display experience in interorganizational collaborations and coalition building.

- Exhibit cultural competency.

- Highlight the strengths of the agency.

3. Project Management and Staffing

- Briefly describe positions needed, including job descriptions and number of full time equivalence (FTE).

- Describe staff recruitment plans that meet the special requirements for the positions.

- Attach resumes of key project staff in appendix. Highlight relevant training and experience.

- Discuss how the project will be managed, e.g.,

    The Project Director will report to the Executive Director and be advised by the 15 persons Project Advisory Board.

    The Project Director will supervise the project which has 3 components via weekly individual and group supervisions. Each component will be staffed by "what kind of people" and be coordinated by a coordinator.

    How often will the project have advisory board meeting, staff meeting, team meeting, individual supervision, training, etc.

Travel cost includes local and out-of-town costs. The federal and state reimbursement rates for mileage or use of personal automobiles changes from time to time. Per-diem rates are also different from city to city. Check the latest listings to ensure the usage of correct rates in the proposal.

Equipment, unlike supplies, refers to items that usually last for several years, and generally are more expensive: program and activity gears, computers, and office furniture. Supplies are items that are less expensive and are disposable after use, such as office supplies, postage, and program incentive materials.

Contractual or consultant costs are for support personnel who are not full-time or part-time employees of the agency. Therefore, they do not receive the aforementioned employee benefits. They may include the external evaluator, tutors, and instructors for the program.

BOX
3.13   **JOB DESCRIPTIONS**

Position Title: Project Director

Position Description: Project Director is responsible for the planning, development, and coordination of the ABC Project, a federally funded substance abuse prevention project. Working under the direction of the Executive Director, the Project Director will oversee the establishment of project services in various program sites.

The **basic responsibilities** are as follows:

1. Administrative: Ensure that guidelines, procedures and program goals, and objectives are met by components. Develop ongoing linkages with the community and the project. Meet and review programs with the ABC Project Advisory Board. Plan and develop programmatic strategies for review by Executive Director and Advisory Board, and implementation by staff.

2. Personnel: Establish administrative and personnel procedures for all managerial and line staff. Develop and implement recruitment and selection procedures for all staff. Assist all project staff in personnel development.

3. Training: Working with project staff to develop and implement a training strategy, curriculum, and program for initial training and ongoing in-service.

4. Management of Grant and Budget: Monitor and review budgetary and fiscal controls and limits. Preparation of monthly and quarterly reports. Ensure reports are submitted regularly by project staff.

5. Evaluation: Coordinate establishment of a management information system (MIS) and evaluate procedures with the evaluation team.

6. Public Relations: Publication and preparation of information to the community and organizations including local, state, and federal authorities; community agencies; and media.

7. Other duties as assigned by the Executive Director.

Minimum Qualifications

1. Graduate degree in health or human services or equivalent experience in nonprofit management.

2. Two or more years in administration of human services with experience in staff, training, program planning and development, budget planning, and report writing.

3. Experience and knowledge of the minority communities in Fine City.

4. Excellent verbal, conceptual, and grammatical skills.

5. Experience in prevention/treatment of substance abuse.

Position Title: Project Counselor

Position Description: The counselor will be developing and providing prevention, education, information, and referral activities to Hispanic youth and their families on issues and problems related to substance abuse and other at-risk behaviors.

The **basic responsibilities** may include the following and are determined by the specific component of which the worker is assigned:

1. Education/Outreach: Assist with high-risk youths and their families through the Community as a Family Center (CFC), schools, community organizations, and activities. Coordinate and implement series of prevention to high-risk youth and their families. Works with media to publicize activities of ABC project.

2. Material Development: Develop bilingual/bicultural educational materials and curriculum. Develop bilingual brochure and flyer aimed at informing at-risk immigrant youth, family, and communities of substance abuse and resources.

3. Youth Center: Develop and lead CFC groups and programs. Coordinate tutoring classes and facilitate parents' participation in center activities.

4. Parenting programs: Coordinate and lead parenting programs. Develop culturally relevant parent- and family-communications activities and materials.

(continued)

BOX
3.13 **JOB DESCRIPTIONS (CONTINUED)**

5. Counseling: Engage and provide individual and group counseling to high-risk youth and their families. Intake and assessment of new clients.

6. Cultural and school programs: Coordinate instructors for cultural activities, and provide support service to Hispanic student at targeted schools.

7. Administration: Ensure adequate record keeping and charting complying with CHAC and ABC policies and procedures. Assist evaluation component in establishing clinical and evaluation procedures. Assist Project Director in meeting goals and objectives. Provide reports as needed.

8. Training: Participate in substance abuse education/cross-cultural counseling training. Assist Project Director in developing training curriculum. Undergo orientation to evaluation procedures.

9. Other duties as assigned by the Executive Director.

Minimum Qualifications

1. BSW or BA in human service disciplines with experience in youth and family counseling or counseling experience.

2. Demonstrated experience in providing human and social services to Hispanic American community.

3. Substance abuse service experience and training preferred.

4. Health/mental health prevention skills in working with high-risk immigrant youth and their families.

5. Strong ability to establish network with community agencies and social systems.

6. Organizational, administrative, and supervisory skills preferred.

7. Bilingual and bicultural in Spanish or Vietnamese preferred.

8. Willingness to flexible hours.

Office space rental could be a very expensive item on the budget, depending on the location of the project in the country. Office construction, including major remodeling, can be an even bigger budget item. Certain funding such as Housing and Urban Development's (HUD) Community Development Block Grant (CDBG) is designed to support construction, while some others may prohibit such expenses. Most funding sources for programming are not interested in construction expenses. Some of them may support leasehold improvement for minor refurbishing work that would make the facility appropriate for implementing the proposed program. Agencies that are interested in construction, equipment, or other major purchases should look to special funding opportunities, foundations, or major fund raising events to get the financial resources.

Items such as printing, staff development, and janitorial service, if not listed as separate items, would make up the catchall item of "Miscellaneous." Applicants should remember that the funding sources are very likely interested in maximizing resources in direct services. It is a good practice to assess the agency's assets and determine whether certain equipment, facilities, space, service capacities/volunteer output, or resources can be spared and be used as "matching funding" or an "in-kind contribution" for the proposed project.

See Box 3.14 for an example of a sample budget.

| BOX 3.14 | SAMPLE OF A FIRST YEAR BUDGET AND JUSTIFICATIONS |

A. Personnel

	Annual Salary	FTE	Months	Cost	Subtotal
Program Director	$50,000	1.0	12	$50,000	
Administrative Assistant	$24,000	0.5	12	$12,000	
Program Coordinators	$36,000	2.0	9	$54,000	
Program Counselors	$30,000	3.0	8	$60,000	
Twelve Month Total					$176,000

B. Benefits (20% of Personnel cost)

1. Payrolls Taxes
2. Employee Benefits
   a. Medical Benefits, b. Dental Benefits, c. Life Insurance
   d. Worker's Compensation Insurance, e. Others

Twelve Month Total	$35,200

C. Indirect Cost (15% of Personnel cost)

	$26,400

D. Travel

1. Take a Break National Conference (2 attendees)	$1,980
a. Airfare and Transportation per Attendee ($500 × 2)	
b. Hotel Accommodation ($110/night × 3 nights × 2)	
c. Per Diem ($40/day × 4 days × 2)	
2. Local (Mileage)	$6,240
a. FTE (Total 8, include 6.5 staff and 1.5 interns/volunteers)	
b. Weekly Mileage/FTE (50 miles)	
c. Number of Work Weeks (48 wks)	
d. Reimbursement Rate ($.325/mile)	
Twelve Month Total	$8,220

E. Equipment

1. Telephone	$3,200
a. 8 Desk Sets: purchase, installation and wiring ($50 × 8 = $400)	
b. Monthly operating cost ($30@ × 12 mo × 8 = $2880)	
2. Personal Computer and Printer	$4,200
a. Number of Computer Sets (3 Sets × $1200)	
b. Number of Printer (2 printers × $300)	
c. Service Contract	
3. Copier Rental	$6,000
a. Unit Cost ($200 × 12 mo = $2,400)	
b. Operation Cost ($3,000 × 12 mo = $3,600)	
4. Office Furniture	$3,200
a. Staff desks and chairs ($150 × 8 = $1,200)	
b. Program tables and chairs, etc. ($2,000)	
Twelve Month Total	$16,600

F. Supplies

1. General Office Supplies ($350 × 12 months)	$4,200
2. XYZ Program/Activity Supplies	$1,200
3. Fax machine	$250
4. Postage ($50/month × 12 months)	$600
5. Program Incentive Materials	$1,000
Twelve Month Total	$7,250

(continued)

**BOX
3.14**   SAMPLE OF A FIRST YEAR BUDGET AND JUSTIFICATIONS (*CONTINUED*)

G. Contractual/Consultants
  1. Program Assistants
     a. Tutors ($10 $\times$ 8 hrs/wk $\times$ 3 tutors $\times$ 40 weeks) $9,600
     b. Interest Club Instructors ($10 $\times$ 8 hrs/wk $\times$ 3 Ins. $\times$ 40 weeks) $9,600
  2. Program Development and Training Consultant $8,000
     ($60/hr $\times$ 100 hrs plus $2,000 per diem and transportation)

Twelve Month Total $27,200

H. Construction
Non-Applicable

I. Office Space
  1. Office Space Rental $72,000
     (3,000 sq. ft. @$2.00/month $\times$ 12 months)
  2. Leasehold Improvement $3,000

Twelve Month Total $75,000

J. Others
  1. Local Conference and Training $1,000
  2. Publications/Printing (3 Brochures and Curricular) $1,500
  3. Janitorial Services $3,000

Twelve Month Total $5,500

Annual Total Budget   **$377,370**

Proposal Reviews

After a program proposal is developed, it is sent to the funding source on or before the deadline for review. Depending on the degree of sophistication of the funding sources, and the size and the seriousness of the funding opportunity, proposals are to be reviewed with different degree of rigors and face different degree of competition.

For most major federal government human service grants, proposal review committees are formed to be responsible for reviews and recommendations regarding all the proposals submitted. These committees consist of experts in the field of practice and representatives from different constituencies. Members in each committee will be asked to review a set of proposals beforehand. Each one of them will be assigned as a primary reader for several proposals, secondary reader and tertiary reader for the other few. During the committee review meeting that may last four to five days, each primary reader will be responsible for presenting the summary of the proposal that he or she is assigned. The reviewer will also give his or her comments and critiques of the proposal. After that, the secondary reader will present his or her comments and highlight the agreements and disagreements with the primary reader. The tertiary reader will then add on his/her comments. Based on the comments from the three readers and each committee member's own readings of the proposal prior to the meeting, the committee will vote and make recommendations to the funding decision makers.

As one can easily point out, this process is rather rigorous. Nevertheless, the effects of the luck of having difficult and detailed readers, or easy readers, are obvious. These assigned readers can be the advocates for the proposal. At the same time, their chosen focuses and comments can direct the discussions into highlighting the weakness and uncertainty of the proposal.

Program planners and proposal writers certainly can take advantage of these review comments to improve their program plans. If the program is not funded, the revised and improved version will be an improved and tested version that will have an increased chance for gaining funding support. Receiving rejection and resubmitting a program proposal is common practice in the human services. Through peer reviews and improvements, programs can become better designed to better serve the needs of clients and communities. Box 3.15 is a sample of a review for a multiyear demonstration grant.

Summary

Grant writing is not only about writing; it involves a lot of planning, organizing, integrating, evaluating, and most importantly critical thinking. The quality of the grant proposal certainly is among the most important factors in funding decisions. Political economy and sheer luck, however, also have their shares in the making of decisions.

This chapter presents a framework for developing a grant proposal, as well as examples. Although it is a labor intensive and challenging endeavor, it is also a most satisfactory undertaking that brings a vision to life and hopefully, when funded, services to the needy. Many years ago, the comic *The Far Side* depicted two little spiders waiting anxiously next to a big spider web at the end of a slide said to each other, "If we pull this off, we'll eat like kings." It is true that writing a good proposal and getting grant funding seems to be an enormous and formidable task. The fact is that many do so and get funded. The first step in getting any grant funding for a service proposal is to submit one. The big catch will eventually come and be caught, only if you have the big web ready to catch it.

To put in a reality check based on our experience, we want to inform you that even after the big grant comes, you—the little spiders—literally will not eat like kings. You will be busy implementing and evaluating what you proposed. At times, you also have doubts that you might have promised too much! However, the actualization of program ideas, and seeing important service providing taking place to meet community needs, are by themselves satisfactory feasts.

References

Barker, R. (Ed.). (1999). *The social work dictionary* (4th ed.). Washington, DC: NASW Press.

Coley, S., & Scheinberg, C. (1990). *Proposal writing*. Newbury, CA: Sage.

Gabor, P., Unrau, Y., & Grinnell, R., Jr. (1998). Evaluation for social workers: A quality improvement approach for the social services (2nd ed.). Boston: Allyn and Bacon.

Netting, F. E., Kettner, P. M., & McMurtry, S. L. (1993). *Social work macro practice*. New York: Longman.

Office for Substance Abuse Prevention (OSAP). (1992). *Three management tools for OSAP demonstration projects for pregnant and postpartum women and their infants (PPWI): Logic models, GOAMS charts, and evaluation plans*. Rockville, MD: Author.

Royse, D., Thyer, B., Padgett, D., & Logan, T. (2001). *Program Evaluation: An introduction.* (3rd ed.). Belmont, CA: Brooks/Cole.

Yuen, F. K. O. (1999). Family health and cultural competency. In Pardeck, J. T., & Yuen, F. K. O. (Eds.). *Family health: A holistic approach to social work practice* (pp. 101–113). Westport, CT: Auburn House.

BOX
3.15   **A SAMPLE PROPOSAL REVIEW**

1. Identification

A. Application Number: 123456789
B. Project Director: Mr. F. Grant, Project Families First.
C. Reviewer's name: Dr. Brightside

2. Description

The Greater Bull Medical Center (GBMC) through its Community and Family Health Center (CFHC) submits an application for a multifaceted project (Families First) for the prevention of alcohol, tobacco, and other drug problems. Families First represents a strong collaboration between CFHC and City Springs School, both located in Bigtown, in east Bull. Anticipated outcomes of Families First include improvements in the physical and emotional health of City Springs' students and their family members, personal skills of students, knowledge of ATOD health risks, family functioning, employability of family members, linkages and communication between families and school personnel, student management, community knowledge of positive health behaviors, and community inputting systems development.

Families First interventions combine activities already in place at City Springs School and CFHC with an array of new activities specifically geared towards improvements in the family and community. Interventions include: Intensive Outreach, Preventive and Primary Health Care for children through the Wellness Center and for family members through CFHC, Peer Mediation, Academic Enrichment, Family/School/Community Events, Brown Bag Lunches and other In-Service Training for school personnel, Community Health Education, involvement in Empowerment Zone Planning, Brothers and Sisters, Family Resource Center, Warm Line, Family Program, Family Needs Assessment, referral to ATOD Treatment, Job Exploration and Job Search, and a Smoking Cessation Program.

3. Critique

The Bull Medical Center's Community and Family Health Center is a well-recognized organization in the community. In cooperation with other health agencies, CFHC has been a provider for primary and preventive health care for the Bigtown community, an identified Empowerment Zone. CFHC has an established relationship with the City Springs School through its current programs on site at the school. The proposed Families First project is a coordinated and comprehensive project and its goals are consistent with identified funding goals. Letters of commitment and support from local organizations attest the resourcefulness of the applicant organization. However, there is no formal indication of support from the School's Parent Teacher Association (volunteers for the Outreach).

The theoretical support for the model of the project is well conceptualized and documented. Statistics cited in the application display the basic demographic information as well as a vivid picture of the depressed socioeconomic situation of the target community. Yet, there is no specific information on the project's target population, e.g., students' health status, school performance, drop-out rate, gang violence, students and family members' involvement with ATOD use, and so on. No data on ATOD use and related issues such as violence and HIV/AIDS in the community are provided. The design of the project seems to rely frequently on the applicant organization's service experience.

Recruitment of participants is to take place on site in the school, in the CFHC, and through home-visits. These trust-building-focused outreach and word-of-mouth approaches are of merit in engaging a hard-to-reach target population. The uses of "Great Grannies" and "Brothers and Sisters" are also consistent with the family focus of the project as well as the community that it intends to serve. Since many of the activities will take place at the school, the Brown Bag Lunch program seems to be a good way to encourage teachers to stay involved in the project.

The proposed project is a comprehensive project and has many project activities. For some of these activities, more details on contents and their implementation are needed. For example, the relationship between the "Wellness Center " and the "Family Resource Center" has not been well defined. Are they the same program? If not, what is the "Wellness Center"? Also, the application indicates that the "You're Special Family Program" will take place twice a week for 1.5 hours each, but there is no discussion on the duration of this activity as well as the follow-up plan for participating parents after they complete the program.

Although the project intends to serve all students in City Springs School (approximately 560 students), the majority of the project activities are focused on students from the 2nd grade to the 4th grade (approximately 250). Since the school serves students from pre-kindergarten to 5th grade, it is not clear how the other students will be served by this project, except through their parents or possible enrollment in the primary and preventive health care program.

The ATOD prevention education program (Bull City Public Schools Health and Family Life Curriculum) includes age-appropriate content and is infused into 2nd to 4th grade curricular. It is, however, not clear whether this curriculum is currently used in the school already. If so, how is it different from the one that is proposed through the application? Also, information on assessing the impact of this curriculum and other Families First programs on the target population is lacking. Overall, there is not sufficient information in the application to indicate the current level of services, and that it is difficult to judge how this project will supplement the existing programs.

The proposed project has a rather comprehensive approach to attract and to serve its target population. This project also utilizes existing resources and links project participants to needed services, including job training, ATOD treatment, and smoking cessation programs. Collaboration and support from other service organizations and commitment from the organization's administration are evident.

The chief evaluator for the application is experienced in education and education technologies. The evaluation plan provides adequate information for both the outcome and process evaluation. No statement of commitment to the funding source's cross-site evaluation is provided.

The proposed project is rather complex and comprehensive; students and their family members can access the program through different activities. While greater access is certainly a strength of the program, this situation also makes it difficult to determine the frequency of target population's participation and the intensity and impact of the interventions. Furthermore, the application lacks measurable outcome objectives and most of the project activity objectives are process objectives. Consequently, the achievement of the funder's goals and the extents of impact of project activities will be hard to assess.

Although students from the Thomas Elementary School will be used as the comparison group for this project and "will be matched with respect to demographics"; no detailed information for this selection and the plan to test the compatibility of the comparison group and the project participants are provided. Additionally, the evaluation plan indicates that the "cross-site analysis" (use of comparison group) will be focusing on "treatment" (p.16). A focus on treatment is inconsistent with the funding source's focus on prevention.

4. Personnel and Management

The management plan for the project is sufficient and the personnel structure is reasonable. The project involves 8 salaried positions (total 6.1 FTE) and volunteers. There is confusion in Section F regarding whether the project director is also the Licensed Clinical Social Worker for the project.

Organizational charts are provided but they do not show how the proposed project will fit into the structure.

5 Budget and Resource

The applicant organization's ability to use existing facilities both within GBMC and City Springs School is a strength of the project.

6. Confidentiality and Other Ethical Concerns

The evaluation plan seems to be in compliance with basic confidentiality and other ethical concerns.

7. Recommendation and Resume

Recommended. Good.

The proposed project is well developed and the application is well written. It has demonstrated the need for an ATOD prevention program in the community and the agency's abilities to deliver such a service building upon its current programs and service network. The cultural competency of the proposed project and its staff are also noted. Unfortunately, the application fails to indicate the agency's current level of services and how the proposed project will supplement its current services. Lack of measurable outcome objectives for activities and evaluation may affect its ability to demonstrate its achievements.

Developing an Evaluation Plan

As program staff start planning for program development and begin addressing the components of the logic model, they should keep in mind that as the logic model takes shape, the development of evaluation plans will follow soon after. The logic model can act as a guide to assist you in determining when your evaluation plan should be developed. As you identify the accomplishments and outcomes in your logic model, the next question to ask yourself is, "How will I determine if I met my accomplishments and reached the outcomes I identified?" The evaluation plan will provide a framework for why the evaluation is to be conducted, what is to be evaluated, and how the evaluation will be conducted. After you have assessed the community needs and determined what services/activities will be implemented to address those needs, the evaluation plan is the next step in your planning process.

Empowerment Evaluation

Before learning how to develop an evaluation plan, it is important to look at the purpose of conducting a program evaluation and understand the type of evaluation models available. This section of the chapter introduces the empowerment evaluation model and the benefits of using this model for program development and improvement.

Gutierrez (1994) defines empowerment as the "process of increasing personal, interpersonal, or political power so that individuals, families, and communities can take action to improve their situations" (p. 202). It is a state of mind of worthiness and control that results in the change of the social and power structure (Swift & Levin, 1987). DuBois and Miley (1996) assert that "empowerment presumes that people themselves should be integrally involved in the change process—from defining their situation to determining goals, selecting their course of action, and evaluating the results" (p. 27). Empowerment evaluation involves program staff as evaluators, fosters their professional development, and promotes self-sufficiency and competency. Fetterman, Kaftarian, and Wandersman (1996), in their definition of the empowerment approach, encourage program staff to be involved in the evaluation development and implementation: "Empowerment evaluation has an unambiguous value orientation—it is designed to help people help themselves and improve their programs using a form of self-evaluation and reflection. Program participants conduct their own evaluations and typically act as facilitators; an outside evaluator often serves as a coach or additional facilitator depending on internal program capabilities" (p. 5). Ginsberg (2001) summarizes the sentiments of the proponents of empowerment evaluation that they see it as a democratic process. It "involves receipts of service in defining the design and implementation as well as the analysis of a program evaluation" (p. 38). Empowerment evaluation promotes participation by all concerned parties and it is considered "comparable to community development or community organization activities in social work" (Ginsberg, 2001, p. 39).

Purpose of Evaluation

Some program administrators have little knowledge about program evaluation and are learning on the job. When asked why one needed to conduct an evaluation, their response was a general statement describing the need to meet compliance by reporting to the funding source on *what occurred in the program.* They prefer not to conduct an evaluation if given the choice, although they are aware that evaluation could assist in improving program services.

A clear understanding of how evaluation can be beneficial for program improvement, prior to implementing a project, can provide program staff with the incentive to take on the task of evaluating their program. To determine the purpose of evaluating their program, program administrators need to identify *what questions they want the evaluation process to answer* as well as *who is asking these questions.* Two other criteria should be considered; first, what resources are available to conduct the evaluation, both in the context of professional expertise as well as funding; and second, how the information will be used. The answers to these questions will assist program staff in planning for their evaluation.

Choosing the Empowerment Evaluation Model

There are a number of types of evaluation models that serve a variety of purposes. Each model has a purpose, and each model plays an important role in the field of evaluation. Therefore, it is important to determine *who* wants to know the answers to *what* questions, and for what *purpose.* The level of resources available also needs to be considered when making these decisions.

When is it appropriate to use empowerment evaluation? The purpose of empowerment evaluation is to assist program staff in conducting a self-assessment of their program services and to use the evaluation results for program improvement. Therefore, the evaluation questions that program staff might ask include:

1. Do the services provided to the community meet the needs identified prior to providing these services?
2. Can the program services be improved so that the quality of services offered to the community increases?

There are three advantages in using the empowerment evaluation. These advantages support the premise of this book that evaluation and program development go hand in hand.

First, because program staff will be involved in conducting the evaluation, the cost of conducting empowerment evaluation will be minimal as compared to contracting with an independent (outside) evaluator.

Second, because program staff are involved in the decisions of what to evaluate and how the evaluation should be conducted, the results will be more meaningful to staff for use in program improvement. Program staff will also be more invested in participating in the evaluation.

Third, the process of developing the evaluation plans forces program staff to take a close look at the program services they intend to provide. As program staff design the plan, they must strategically lay out the community needs, activities to address the needs, target population to be served, and the desired outcome of the services provided. At this point of the evaluation development process, program staff can begin to see if the steps "align," or support, one another. For example, will the activity address the need? Is the population to be served a part of the need? Will the desired outcome occur as a result of the activity?

However, one must not overlook the challenge program staff face when choosing to use the empowerment evaluation approach. Because program staffs are taking a large role in conducting the evaluation, two hurdles stand before them:

1. Program staff may have little knowledge and/or experience in designing and conducting an evaluation. They may need assistance from a professional evaluator and the willingness to learn how to conduct their own self-assessment of program services. Attitude toward learning how to conduct an evaluation using the empowerment approach is critical to the success of implementation.
2. Program staff are given an added responsibility, in addition to program implementation. They must also be responsible for conducting the evaluation of program services. This places an added burden on a staff's already busy schedule. There are two approaches that can ease this burden. First, to the extent possible, program staff can infuse the evaluation tasks as part of the program delivery. Second, the more program staff accept the evaluation tasks as being a necessary part of the overall program service effort, the less burdensome the tasks will seem. Again, attitude toward evaluation plays a critical role in the quality of evaluation conducted.

As described above, program staff are conducting their own evaluation, including collecting their own data and, in some cases, making subjective decisions in determining whether or not gain has occurred. Because this is a self-assessment, program staff must maintain a high standard of integrity. If staff want to, they can manipulate the data to make their program look successful, regardless of the actual outcomes. However, this would defeat the purpose of conducting an empowerment evaluation. Therefore, the need to revisit the purpose of this evaluation approach is important. The evaluation results are to be used for program improvement. If staff choose to manipulate the data (e.g., information being collected), the evaluation results may be meaningless and not helpful for program improvement.

The Evaluation Plan

What is an evaluation plan, when should this plan be fully developed, and who should develop the plan? Using the empowerment evaluation approach, program staff enagage in developing an evaluation plan for their programs.

Program staff understand how to develop and implement services to meet the needs of the community. Some of them may not have the knowledge or experience to determine how the program will be evaluated. Certain program staff rely on "others" to design evaluation plans and conduct an evaluation while they attend to program issues. However, the empowerment approach does not follow this model.

In a perfect world, program staff will begin to view empowerment evaluation as a necessary part of the program delivery. For example, in an after-school tutoring program, just as the program would not be functional if tutors did not tutor students, so would the program not be functional if an evaluation was not conducted to measure desired outcomes for program improvement.

This chapter will describe incidents of how community organizations, local governmental agencies, educational systems, and faith-based organizations implemented the empowerment evaluation approach. The benefits of this approach, the burden placed on the programs, and how the evaluation approach can be infused with program development or improvement will also be discussed.

FIVE STEPS IN DEVELOPING AND IMPLEMENTING EMPOWERMENT EVALUATION

1. Develop an evaluation plan.
2. Identify or develop measurement tools.
3. Collect the data.
4. Analyze the data.
5. Report evaluation results.

A five-step approach is recommended to use for the development and implementation of program evaluation (see Box 4.1). The first of these five steps is the development of an evaluation plan.

Why Develop an Evaluation Plan?

When implementing program services, it is good practice to have a plan before proceeding. Usually the grant proposal serves this purpose. In the case of implementing process and outcome evaluations, evaluation plans also serve this purpose. The evaluation plan describes what the evaluation will look like and what information will be collected. Plans can be developed in a number of different formats, from an outline framework to detailed text. The outline format is particularly useful when using the empowerment approach in developing an evaluation plan and having the expectation of program staff to participate in its design.

Evaluation plans serve both as a guide for program staff to conduct the evaluation, as well as a means to show stakeholders what is to be evaluated and how the evaluation will be conducted. There are two basic types of evaluation plans; one plan will serve those programs that want to conduct a project-wide evaluation, and the second plan will serve those programs that want to utilize an objective-oriented evaluation. Examples of evaluation plans appear in Chapter 7.

When Should the Evaluation Plan Be Developed?

Typically, as program staff begin to conduct their program planning and implementation, the thought of evaluating program services does not occur until the end of a program delivery cycle, or when a program report must be developed. Subsequently, the write-ups about the evaluation are vague. In some cases, they reflect the staff's lack of knowledge and understanding of the utilities and feasibility of evaluation. Ideally, the evaluation plan should be developed as the proposal is being written, or a detailed evaluation plan should be developed after the program design has been established but before the implementation of services begins.

The process of developing the evaluation plan will help form the direction and design of the program as well as clarify the purpose of conducting the activity or service. The authors have assisted many community-based programs in developing evaluation plans using the objective-oriented evaluation approach. When developing an evaluation plan, the one burning question that forces program staff to take a second look at how they are conducting their program services is:

What are you hoping the participants will gain or change after having participated in your services?

Having a clear vision of what the desired result will be after services are provided can help program staff carefully decide how they plan to implement their services (see Box 4.2). This process provides program staff with an opportunity to again question whether or not the program services planned will, in fact, provide the information, experience, or skills to participants, so that the desired result is reached.

Who Should Be Involved in the Development of the Evaluation Plan?

The empowerment approach stresses the need for program staff and stakeholders to become involved in the design and implementation of the evaluation plan. Both program staff and key stakeholders are encouraged to be involved in the development of the evaluation plan. This is one of the places where they have the opportunity to have a say in what they want to evaluate and how best to conduct the evaluation. They will more likely be invested in supporting the evaluation, and in some cases conducting the evaluation, because they will be obtaining information they can use to help improve the services they offer, determine if the type of services provided are appropriate to meet the community needs, and justify the good work they are providing. As demonstrated in Box 4.2, when program staff know what desired change is wanted, they will be more inclined to design and implement services that will focus on those desired changes.

The ability to demonstrate a change in a situation when services are to prevent negative results from occurring can be challenging. Some program staff that have implemented community services have demonstrated the ability to conduct process evaluation, documenting the accomplishments of services provided. However, they may not have the knowledge or experience to design a detailed evaluation plan without assistance, especially when developing an outcome evaluation plan for prevention services. Over time, program staff will develop skills in preparing and implementing an evaluation plan.

How Should the Evaluation Plan Be Designed?

Evaluation plans can be multifaceted, consisting of a variety of detailed information. On the other hand, evaluation plans can provide the essential information needed to conduct a basic evaluation. We have found that developing an evaluation plan using a framework design for why, when and how to conduct an evaluation works well when facilitating program staff to conduct their own evaluation.

In developing an evaluation plan, there is no "one way" to proceed. There are many options that can be used. However, the framework approach is very simple yet provides the detailed information needed to guide program staff through the implementation. It makes sense to the program staff and the results can be effectively used for program improvement. This model will also provide information that can be used for other purposes, such as quality assurance or writing grant proposals.

As demonstrated in Chapter 3, the grant proposal defines the need for the service, the type of service/activity proposed that will respond to the need, the resources (input) needed to implement the program, the accomplishments (output) expected to be achieved, and the benefits (outcomes) anticipated as a result of the services provided by program staff. The evaluation plan may include a synopsis of this information as well as additional information on how accomplishment data will be collected and what outcome data will be collected.

BOX
4.2   AFTER-SCHOOL PROGRAM FOR ELEMENTARY STUDENTS

Many of the after-school programs offered academic support or recreational activities and had a general "purpose statement" regarding why they implemented those services (e.g., have a supervised place where youth can go). Although the services they offered served a purpose and, in many cases, their programs provided youth with specific cognitive, intellectual, social, or emotional benefits, there was a lack of focus on specific outcome gains. Developing an evaluation plan helped program staff improve their program by focusing their recreational services so that the youth had opportunities to develop knowledge or skills in a social/emotional area or cognitive/intellectual area.

For example, program staff decided to focus their recreational activities to teach youth how to handle conflict in a constructive manner as youth participated in these recreational activities. Therefore, program staff planned conflict resolution training for themselves so that they could model appropriate methods of resolving conflict when conflicts arose between youths during recreational play. Program staff also discussed structuring the recreational activities so that youth would have the opportunity to use conflict resolution skills in organizing recreational activities, developing rules, or becoming team leaders.

Types of Evaluation Plans

The Project-Wide Evaluation Plan and the Objective-Oriented Evaluation Plan are the two types of evaluation plans that have many utilities for human service program.

Project-Wide Evaluation Plan

When developing an evaluation plan for a project that looks at the broad goals of the project, an evaluation plan format that provides a "big picture" outline is suggested. For the sake of identifying this approach, it will be called the Project-Wide Evaluation Plan.

One of the first steps in developing this type of evaluation plan is to identify the "big" questions that the evaluation is to answer. After these Evaluation Questions have been developed, one must determine the sources that will be used to provide the information that will answer these questions. For example, in a tutoring program, if the big question is whether or not students increase their literacy skills, the source of information can be the students, teachers, parents, or tutors. After identifying where the source of information will be retrieved, the next step to address is how this information will be collected, or what evaluation method will be used to collect this information. For example, will students be tested, will teachers complete a survey, will parents be interviewed, or will the tutors document progress throughout the school year as they provide tutoring services? Box 4.3 demonstrates what a typical project-wide evaluation plan might look like. The type of descriptions in each of the columns can vary, and the number of columns can expand or be reduced, depending on how detailed the evaluation plan is to be developed.

Objective-Oriented Evaluation Plan

The sections that make up an objective-oriented evaluation plan are stated below. Keep in mind that the plan should address two focus areas: accomplishments or process evaluation, and benefits to the recipients of service or outcome evaluation. For a clear picture of the components of an objective-oriented evaluation plan, see Box 4.4.

BOX 4.3	TYPICAL PROJECT-WIDE EVALUATION PLAN

Evaluation Question	Source of Information	Method	Timeline	Responsible Person

BOX 4.4	SAMPLE EVALUATION PLAN COMPONENTS FOR AN OBJECTIVE-ORIENTED EVALUATION

1. Community need
2. Activity or service to be implemented
3. Desired result
4. Indicators (elements to be measured/collected)
5. Method of measurement
6. Type of instrument to be used
7. Minimum level of success the program hopes to achieve
8. The implementation steps
   A. Who is going to collect the data?
   B. When will the data be collected (dates/timeline)?
   C. Who will be responsible for aggregating and analyzing the data?
   D. How will the results be used, and who will be responsible for determining the format for use of the results?
   - Reports
   - Reflection
   - Public relations
   - Fundraising
   - Other uses of the results

This framework can be used to develop both the process evaluation as well as the outcome evaluation. However, if desired, an evaluation plan can be developed for each of these areas. Let us first focus on developing an evaluation plan that includes both the process evaluation and outcome evaluation. Again, process evaluation will answer the question, "Did you do what you said you were going to do?" The outcome evaluation will answer questions such as, "What benefits did the recipients of service obtain?", and "How well did you do?"

Developing an Evaluation Plan that Includes Process Evaluation and Outcome Evaluation

Process and outcome evaluation are the first two common areas of focus for the empowerment evaluation approach. A third focus area is impact evaluation, the long-term effects that have occurred as a result of the services provided. This latter focus area tends to be more complicated and, many times, requires professional assistance.

Project-Wide Evaluation Plan

For each "big" evaluation question, determine whether you are going to conduct a process evaluation, outcome evaluation, or both. Identify sources of whom and from where the information will be provided, and methods of how the information will be collected. Remember that process evaluation requires the documentation of accomplishments made, while outcome evaluation requires the gathering of information from a variety of possible sources that indicate benefits were achieved as a result of the services provided. Next, identify a timeline when the information will be collected and the person responsible for collecting the data. For a detailed example, see Box 4.5.

There is no limit to the number of "big" questions to ask. However, the more questions asked, the more effort program staff will need to make to answer the questions. Therefore, keep the number of "big" questions to a minimum, those that will provide information for program improvement, quality assurance, or other necessary qualifications.

Objective-Oriented Evaluation Plan

For those developing objective-oriented evaluation plans from a grant proposal, the proposal should already have information describing the needs, the services that are being proposed to address the needs, and the accomplishments and desired results anticipated as a result of the services provided. In the spirit of program improvement, here is an opportunity to revisit the services being offered and discuss whether or not these services need to be modified, expanded, or eliminated. This information will be used as part of the evaluation plan. The next steps will be to determine the data needed and how these data will be collected so that the evaluation will demonstrate whether or not the accomplishments and outcomes have been met. The Objective and Evaluation Plan Development Form (see Box 3.11 on page 35) lists the major components and steps in designing and implementing evaluation strategies for an objective. The following sections of this chapter provide descriptions and examples of each of the key components.

BOX 4.5   SAMPLE PROJECT-WIDE EVALUATION PLAN

Evaluation Question	Source of Information	Method	Timeline	Responsible Person
To what extent did the students increase their literacy skills after having participated in the after-school literacy tutoring program?	Number of students served at least 10 weeks, 3 sessions per week.	Student Participant Log (*process*)	Ongoing	Tutors
				Project Director
	Students' achievement	Assessment tests	August (obtain results)	Project Director
	Teachers' attitudes	Survey		
	Parents attitudes	Interviews		Site Coordinator
Do students have a more positive attitide towards school after they participate in the tutoring program?	Principal	Interviews	May	Project Director
	Teachers	Survey	May	Project Director

Need A description of the service need should already be described in the grant proposal or mission statement of existing services. A brief statement of the need would suffice here (see Box 4.6). If this particular objective focuses on a specific area of need of the grant proposal, state only the specific area that will be addressed as a result of implementing the activity or service. For example, if an after-school enrichment program's particular evaluation plan focuses only on youth leadership services, only these services need to be described, even if the program will also offer arts and crafts to increase cultural identity, and recreational activities to increase social skills.

Activity or Service This section should state who is providing the service, what service is provided, where the service is offered, when the service is offered, and how often the service is offered. Using the example previously described, if this objective is focused on the mentoring program, provide information only on the mentoring efforts (see Box 4.7). Do not discuss the arts and crafts activities or the recreational activities.

Beneficiaries The number of beneficiaries and the characteristics of the beneficiaries should be discussed here. The type of characteristics can determine the challenges program staff will face when providing services. For example, the number of students participating in the mentoring program should be discussed here, as well as any characteristics, such as students who have behavioral problems or introverted students, which may affect the outcomes of services provided (see Box 4.8). Again, this information should already be described in the grant proposal.

 BOX 4.6   **STATEMENT OF NEED**

Need	**Example**
Describe the need in the community that will be addressed by proposed services.	Over 50% of the students in Wayne County School District come from single-parent family homes whose parents hold full-time jobs. Negative attitudes of students in grades 3–8 toward educational achievement have become a major concern over the last three years as indicated by increased truancy and disrespectful behavior.

BOX 4.7   **DESCRIPTION OF ACTIVITY OR SERVICE**

Activity or Service	**Example**
Describe the service activity you will be evaluating (who will do what, when, and where).	Fifty senior citizen volunteers, trained to become mentors, will be placed at five Wayne County elementary schools, ten per school, to provide one-on-one mentoring to third and fourth grade students; each mentor will be matched with two students for the entire school year, meeting with each student three times per week, 30 minutes per session, during after-school hours on school campus.

DISCUSSION OF BENEFICIARIES

Beneficiaries	**Example**
Briefly describe the people (and estimated number) your activity will serve.	100 third and fourth grade students in Wayne County School District who demonstrate poor attitudes toward school and disrespect toward peers and school staff, identified by school administration.

Desired Accomplishments Accomplishments, as process data, are the actions and numbers that occurred during the implementation of the program. These are the elements that can be documented to answer whether the program actually did what was stated in the proposal. For example, in a mentoring program, the accomplishments to be collected may include:

- Number of youth matched with an adult mentor.
- Number of mentors who completed the training and were matched with a youth.
- Number of mentors who completed their mentor commitment.
- Number of youth who followed through with participating in the mentor program.
- Frequency and amount of time (i.e., minutes, hours) mentors and youth met.

The accomplishments described above can answer the question of whether or not the program provided the services to the degree it stated it would in the proposal (see Box 4.9).

Desired Result Desired result, as outcome data, is the big picture of what is hoped for as a result of providing services to the beneficiaries (see Box 4.10). The desired result may or may not be reachable within the timeline of the evaluation cycle (e.g., annual evaluation); however, if the services continue for an extended period of time, the result could be realized.

Indicators Indicators are the elements that are documented and counted to determine if the services provided were actually fulfilling what was proposed in the proposal (see Box 4.11). These elements are the changes that can be reached within the timeline of the evaluation cycle and, if continued over an extended period of time, will lead to the desired result. For example, if the proposal stated that the mentoring program would increase youth leadership skills, what indicators will be documented to determine if the youth did in fact increase their skills? Examples of indicators include:

- Becoming more involved in school and/or community projects.
- Becoming a role model for other youth.
- Willingness to do tasks when not having to do those tasks.

Method of Measurement This section should describe the method to be used to document the desired accomplishments and desired results (see Box 4.12). For process evaluation, determining a method to document accomplishments usually involves tallying or keeping a record of what occurs. For example, the method of process measurement for a mentoring program may include:

DESIRED ACCOMPLISHMENTS

Desired Accomplishments

Describe what type and quantity of services you hope to provide (e.g., number of times met, time providing service, length of the program services).

Example

50 senior citizen volunteers will complete the training, and each volunteer will mentor two students for the entire school year, meeting with each student three times per week.

RECORD OF DESIRED RESULTS

Desired Results

Explain what outcome changes will occur because of the described activity.

Example

Increased positive academic performance in school.

LIST OF INDICATORS

Indicators

Describe the concrete, observable indicators of progress toward your outcome desired result.

Example

Increased participation in school activities and academic performance; as well as increased respect towards school personnel and peers.

DOCUMENTING METHODS OF MEASUREMENT

Method of Measurement

Describe the method you will use to determine if the described change occurs.

Example

Process: Volunteer mentors will document sessions held with assigned students.

Outcome: Project director will interview the school administration regarding student performance in academic achievement, participation in school activities, and respect towards school personnel/peers.

- Tallying the number of mentors recruited, by documenting how many completed the training and how many were matched with a youth, the number of times participated in support group meetings or special mentor/mentee events and completed their commitment to be a mentor, and determining the number willing to continue as a mentor after their initial commitment.
- Tallying the number of youth agreeing to participate in the mentor program, times keeping commitments with their mentor, number of times/hours meeting with the mentor, completed the commitment as a mentee.
- Number of support groups held and number of mentors attending each meeting, number of special events held and number of mentors/mentee teams participating in each event.

For outcome evaluation, determining a method to document indicators can consist of conducting observations, administering surveys, holding focus groups or interviews, or collecting existing data. For example, the method of an outcome measurement for a mentoring program may include surveying youth to determine their attitudes toward becoming involved in school and community activities, or conducting focus groups with mentors to determine how they observed changes in the leadership skills of the youth they mentored.

Type of Instruments   The forms needed to document the elements for process evaluation generally include tally forms and attendance sheets (see Box 4.13). These forms are very basic and do not require much effort in developing. However, all too often program staff do not use forms; they just use papers that happen to be available to document the needed information. While this is acceptable because the information is indeed being collected, it is not an organized and concerted effort to collect useful data. As basic as a tally form or attendance sheet may be to develop, having "official forms" to collect these data is important for the following reasons:

- As basic as the information needed for each form (e.g., date, name of participant, location, type of event), a form acts as a "standard" for requiring staff to complete the required data.
- A form looks official; this places more emphasis on the importance of this information and the need to collect it on a regular basis.
- If different people are completing these forms, having the same forms keeps the data collection in an organized fashion.

When identifying instruments to collect "indicator" information for the outcome evaluation, program staff may not yet have identified an instrument, or may need to develop an instrument to meet their needs. However, program staff should still state, as detailed as possible, the type of instrument they plan to use. Examples of instrument descriptions can include a Pre-Post Student Leadership Attitude Survey or a Mentor Focus Group Protocol.

Standard of Success   When writing a proposal and identifying the number of beneficiaries to serve, the efforts to accomplish, or the level of change wanted, the ability to meet these proposed accomplishments and desired results may or may not be reachable. The grant proposal is just that, a proposal; the information is what you hope to accomplish. There may be many situations that prevent program staff from implementing the service as intended. Therefore, when developing your evaluation plan, include what you hope to accomplish minimally (see Box 4.14). Using the information stated in their proposal, program staff have the opportunity to set minimum standards they hope the program to reach. For example, a mentoring program may want to have a minimum of 90% of the mentors complete the training, and 80% of those trained complete their

BOX 4.13   LISTING TYPES OF INSTRUMENTS

Types of Instruments	Example
Describe the instrument(s) that you will use.	*Process:* Volunteer mentor session documentation form
	Outcome: Teacher Interview Protocol on student mentee participation and respect for others

BOX 4.14   MINIMAL STANDARDS

Standard of Success	Example
Define the minimum level of success you hope to achieve.	*Process:* 90% of the senior citizen mentor volunteers will complete their training.
	Outcome:
	a. 70% of the students will increase their participation in school academics and activities.
	b. 80% will become more respectful to school personnel and peers.

mentor commitment. The standard for its outcome evaluation may be to have minimally 70% of the youth participating in the mentoring program to increase their leadership skills.

Respondents and Measurements Schedule   The respondents to be identified here are the persons completing the instrument (see Box 4.15). This does not necessarily mean that the recipients of service will always be the respondents. For example, if youth participating in a mentoring program complete a survey, they would be the respondents; if the mentors complete a survey, they would be the respondents; if the supervisory staff completed an observational checklist on confidence skills, they would be the respondents. Also include the dates when the instruments are to be completed.

Data Collection, Data Aggregation, and Data Analysis   The next three elements should list the persons who will be responsible for data collection, data aggregation, and data analysis (see Box 4.16). These people may not necessarily be the people who conduct the tasks; however, they are the persons that need to make sure the tasks are conducted in a timely manner, the tasks are completed, and the instruments are secured and in a confidential location. Ideally, a person's name is listed for each of these tasks; however, at the very least, the title or specific position is identified and stated for these tasks. To list *program staff* as the responsible persons for any of these tasks is too vague. One person needs to be identified and held accountable.

BOX 4.15   RESPONDENTS AND MEASUREMENTS SCHEDULE

Respondents and Measurements Schedule	Example
Describe who will be completing each instrument and the schedule for completing the instrument(s).	*Process:* 50 volunteer mentors will document the dates and length of time of each mentoring session. *Outcome:* Teachers at each of the five schools will participate in quarterly interviews regarding student participation in academics, activities, and respect.

BOX 4.16   RESPONSIBLE PERSONS FOR DATA COLLECTION, DATA AGGREGATION, AND DATA ANAYSIS

Data Collection	Example
Describe who will collect the data and how often it will be collected.	*Process:* Site coordinators will be responsible for collecting the process evaluation data weekly. *Outcome:* The project director will be responsible for collecting the outcome evaluation data quarterly.

Data Aggregation	Example
Describe who will be responsible for aggregating the data and how often will it be aggregated.	*Process:* Each site coordinator will aggregate the process evaluation data for their school site at the end of each semester (January and May) and submit the data to the project director. *Outcome:* Project director will compile the interview data quarterly.

Data Analysis	Example
Describe who will be responsible for analyzing the data.	The project director will analyze the process evaluation data received from the five site coordinators; project director will analyze the outcome data at the end of each semester.

Reporting Results   The last element of the evaluation plan is to identify the responsible person that will be writing the evaluation report (see Box 4.17). Many times, the person responsible for the aggregation and analysis is the same person responsible for reporting the results. More than one report may be planned or required; therefore, due dates should also be listed here so that the person responsible will know when the data collection, aggregation, and analysis need to be completed, allowing time for the report to be completed by the deadline dates.

This description on developing an evaluation is very basic, yet provides the necessary information to plan and conduct the evaluation. Examples of evaluation plans can be found at the end of Chapter 5, "The Strategies and Tools for Data Collection."

> **BOX**
> **4.17** **RESPONSIBLE PERSON FOR REPORTING RESULTS**

Reporting Results	Example
Describe who will be responsible for writing the report and how often will reports be due.	The project director will write the evaluation report in October and conduct an oral presentation before the Board of Education during the first quarter of the next school year.

Attached to each evaluation plan is the instrument identified for that particular evaluation plan. When reviewing the evaluation plan, observe how the instrument identified supports the plan in the areas of desired result, indicators, method of measure, and respondents. Also, look at how the standard of success is stated and the type of data collected. The type of data collected should answer whether or not the standard of success has been met.

Summary

Developing an evaluation plan is the first of five steps (see Box 4.1 on page 49) in setting up and conducting an evaluation of community services. A number of evaluation models exist; each has an important role in the research and evaluation field. Choosing the appropriate evaluation model to meet the stakeholders' needs determines how the evaluation will be developed and who will develop the plan.

This chapter describes the empowerment evaluation approach in conducting both a process evaluation and outcome evaluation of program services. The primary purpose of this approach is to use the evaluation results for continuous program improvement. Program staffs become involved in the planning, decision making, and implementation of the empowerment evaluation. Both the process of developing the evaluation plan, as well as implementation of the evaluation plan, contributes to the knowledge base and experience for improving program services.

References

DuBois, B. & Miley, K. K. (1996). *Social work: An empowering profession* (2nd ed.). Needham Heights, MA: Allyn & Bacon.

Fetterman, D. M., Kaftarian, S. J., & Wandersman, A. (1996). *Empowerment evaluation: Knowledge and tools for self-assessment and accountability.* Thousand Oaks, CA: Sage.

Ginsberg, L. H. (2001). *Social work evaluation: Principles and methods.* Boston: Allyn and Bacon.

Gutierrez, L. M. (1994). Beyond coping: An empowerment perspective on stressful life events. *Journal of Sociology and Social Welfare, 21,* 201–219.

Swift, C., & Levin, G. (1987). Empowerment: An emerging mental health technology. *Journal of Primary Prevention, 8,* 71–94.

Witkin, B. R., Altschuld, J. W. (1995). *Planning and conducting needs assessments: A practical guide.* Thousand Oaks, CA: Sage.

Wolcott, H. F. (1991). *Writing up qualitative research.* Thousand Oaks, California: Sage.

The Strategies and Tools for Data Collection

Many evaluation consultants report that one of the first things that programs tend to request is the identification of evaluation tools (see Box 5.1). Program staff generally make these requests toward the end of their program year after providing the services. Some of them are not aware of the evaluation process. Meanwhile, some others may have conducted inappropriate or invalid evaluation tasks.

Before focusing on the type of tools for data collection, program staffs need to revisit the objectives and evaluation plan, and then consider the data collection strategies and the tools to select/develop for data collection.

Objectives Revisited

Before discussing the data collection strategies and instruments to collect the data, let's revisit the objectives stated in the grant proposal. Strong program objectives describe the services to be provided and who will benefit from the services. It should also describe the desired results, how the services will be measured, and what the program hopes to achieve. The objectives should have specific information about the services to be delivered so that, when evaluated, program staff can determine if the objectives have or have not been met (Netting, Kettner, & MxMurtry, 1993; Gabor, Unrau, & Grinnell, 1998).

When the authors assisted programs that the federal Corporation for National Service funded, a simple guide was used to assist program staff review their objectives and determine if all of the information was included. This guide was used in reviewing objectives prior to assisting programs develop evaluation plans and implementation strategies. If the objectives are clear and detailed, developing evaluation plans, identifying instruments, and collecting the data will be much easier. Consider the questions raised in Box 5.2 when reviewing your objectives.

Writing clear objectives will contribute to a strong grant proposal. It will also provide a solid foundation for developing an evaluation plan. The more complete the objective, the easier it will be to develop and implement an evaluation plan. As the process of developing and implementing each of the five evaluation steps (see Box 4.1 on page 49) are discussed, it will be apparent that each step builds upon and supports the previous steps of the evaluation process.

Evaluation Plan Revisited

The empowerment evaluation approach encourages program staff to be the facilitators of their own evaluation. Program staffs become primary players in the contribution of evaluation content and methods as they develop the evaluation plan. Included in the evaluation plan are the data collection strategies and identification of instruments. As program staffs enter these next

---

<table>
<tr><td>**BOX**
5.1</td><td>**FIRST REQUEST WHEN ASKING FOR EVALUATION ASSISTANCE**</td></tr>
</table>

"I have a mentoring program, please send me a survey on self-esteem."

"Please send me some type of measure to evaluate the effectiveness of the parenting programs for teen moms."

<table>
<tr><td>**BOX**
5.2</td><td>**COMPONENTS OF A MEASURABLE OBJECTIVE**</td></tr>
</table>

1. In describing the activity: Is the activity clearly defined? Who will provide the services? When and how often will this activity occur? Where will the activity be conducted?

   Example: Fifty adult volunteers, trained in literacy tutoring, will be placed at five elementary schools, ten per school, to provide one-on-one literacy tutoring to third and fourth grade students; each tutor will tutor six students per week during the entire school year, meeting with each student four times per week, 30 minutes per session, during school hours.

2. In defining the result: What is the desired overarching accomplishments or outcomes you hope to see as a result of providing the services in your program?

   Example: Increased student literacy skills.

3. In determining how to measure the results: What type of instruments do you anticipate using and what methods do you plan to conduct to measure both accomplishments and outcomes?

   Example: Accomplishments—Volunteer Tutors will document the sessions held with assigned students. Outcomes—Standardized test scores in reading of last school year will serve as the baseline and standardized test scores in reading taken at the end of the school year will serve as the post-test.

4. In describing what you hope to achieve: What, minimally do you want to accomplish or occur as a result of your services? Ideally, we would like to have a 100% of whatever it is we want to accomplish or occur; however, in most cases, this is not realistic.

   Example: Accomplishments—80% of the adult tutors will meet with their assigned students at least 90% of the scheduled tutoring sessions. Outcomes—70% of the students will increase their standardized test scores in reading by at least 0.5 of a grade level.

5. In describing the beneficiaries: How many recipients will be served (be realistic, consider the resources to provide the service). Do the recipients have social issues or needs (e.g., homeless people, English as a second language participants, truant youth) or will the beneficiaries be something other than people (e.g., animals, plants, or other environmental issues)?

   Example: 300 third and fourth grade students in five elementary schools who scored at least two grades below grade level in their standardized reading test.

---

two steps of the evaluation process, the evaluation plan becomes a reference to guide program staff in a consistent direction. This reference will help program staff keep the evaluation process in alignment. When the discussion of data collection strategies and identification of instruments are presented, references to the evaluation plan will be made throughout this chapter.

A Guideline for Data Collection Strategies and Developing Instruments

In developing an evaluation plan, program evaluators would identify the types of instruments to be used, the methods of conducting the evaluation, and the persons who will be completing the instruments or provide the data. The evaluation plan functions as a roadmap that provides the direction for how the evaluation is to be developed and implemented. After the plan has been completed, specific instrument or instruments need to be identified or develop. Also, data collection strategies need to be planned and arranged so that the logistics of collecting the data will operate smoothly.

As program staffs and program evaluators move forward in these next two tasks, the evaluation plan will help them to maintain alignment of their evaluation. Program staffs are encouraged to refer to their plan periodically so that they do not divert the evaluation planning efforts in a different direction. Will the instruments identified provide the information needed to determine if the desired result has been met? Can the instruments be used in accordance with the data collection strategies being planned? Are the data collection strategies achievable considering the type of activity to be conducted and the characteristics of beneficiaries to be served? These are a few questions that program staffs need to ask themselves so that they maintain alignment in the implementation of their evaluation.

Data Collection Strategies and Identifying Instruments

The evaluation plan provides direction for the type of instruments needed and how they will be used (i.e., methodology). The evaluation plan also describes who is going to provide the data (e.g., complete the instruments), when the data needs to be collected, and who is the responsible person that will see that the data is collected. Each of these two evaluation steps, data collection strategies and identification of instruments, need to be undertaken simultaneously. Changing the elements of one can affect the functionality of the other. Therefore, before each of these steps can be finalized, working on these steps lends itself to going back and forth until both support and are compatible with one another.

Instruments

A measurement tool is a specific instrument for collecting and documenting information about the results of your service (e.g., a public safety survey, a reading skills rubric, pre-post parenting skills test, a life skills observational checklist). Be sure to always connect your measurement tools to your activity, indicators, and results. For instance, if you want to evaluate an improvement in reading skills, a log to collect information on homework completion would not measure increased reading skills; however, a pre-post reading inventory would. In addition, be sure that you are able to access the type of information you need. For example, it may be difficult to get student grades because of confidentiality policies of the school district; however, you may be able to survey teachers on student progress.

When should program staff select existing instruments to evaluate their program, and when should they develop their own instruments? Begin by reviewing the evaluation plan. What instruments are stated in the plan? Who will be completing the instruments? What are the desired results and indicators that are hoped to be achieved? These questions are critical to determining the identification of an appropriate instrument. Remember that empowerment evaluation is in use, and the program staff make the decisions on what to evaluate and how should the evaluation be conducted.

Selecting Existing Instruments

An existing instrument may already exist that can be used to evaluate the program services implemented. Therefore, program staff may want to investigate whether or not they can identify an instrument that would meet their needs before considering developing their own instrument. There are advantages in using an existing instrument over developing instruments. Where does one look to find these instruments? What are the elements to be considered when selecting the instrument? How does one know that the instrument selected is appropriate for the evaluation conducted?

If the right instrument is selected and used correctly, the data collected can accurately reflect what is to be measured, particularly in comparison with other programs using the same instruments, and the validity and reliability of the instrument may be tested. However, program staff need to respond to two questions: "Where do I look to determine if an instrument exists that measures what the program hopes to evaluate?" and "What do I look for in an instrument to determine if the instrument is measuring the desired result of my services I am providing?"

There are a number of resources that program staff can turn to respond to the first question. Program staff can talk with research and evaluation professionals (e.g., university faculty and staff, research firms), look for existing community programs providing the same type of service and investigate what instruments they are using to evaluate their services, conduct a search in a library (ideally a university library), contact a national clearinghouse that focuses on the type of service being offered, or search the Internet.

For standardized or clinical assessments, the late Walter Hudson, a social work educator and researcher, and his associates have produced a number of scales that can be found in several publications (Nurius & Hudson, 1993; Nugent, Sieppert, & Hudson, 2001). Corcoran and Fischer (1999a, 1999b), among other researchers, also published books that have scales and instruments for various evaluations and assessments. In the fields of education, psychology, and public health, one could also find many existing scales and instruments.

After program staff have conducted a broad search for existing instruments and identify a few that indicate they will measure what is hoped to be evaluated, program staff still need to take a more detailed look at the instruments. To answer the second question, staff needs to make sure the ones selected align with the program services provided, the measurements of the beneficiaries, the timeline when results can be realized, and the intended use of the data (see Box 5.3). Many established or validated instruments are copyrighted or are for commercial use. Getting permissions from authors and paying for the cost for administering the instruments may be required. Box 5.4 describes the elements to be considered in selecting off-the-shelf instruments.

When program staff search for and select an existing instrument, they also need to keep in mind whether or not these instruments come with existing administrative guidelines or manuals that may require training or professional expertise to administer the instruments. In some cases, if the requirements on how to use the instrument are not followed, the data collected may not be valid or reliable as per the intent of the instrument. One should also check the instrument directions to find out if the following instructions exist:

BOX 5.3 **METHODS NOT TO USE WHEN IDENTIFYING INSTRUMENTS**

The project director of an after-school program wants to decrease alcohol or other drug abuse of youth by increasing student's self-esteem, focusing on strengthening resiliency traits of youth. The project director uses an instrument titled, "Youth Self-Esteem Assessment" because the word "self-esteem" is in the title of the assessment. However, the program offers tutoring to increase students' attitude towards school, a resiliency trait that associates with and may contribute to the increase in self-esteem of youth. This instrument only measures self-esteem in general and may not measure attitude towards school.

Caution: This instrument may not align with the services measured. Positive attitude towards school is a resiliency trait that contributes to increased self-esteem and can contribute to the prevention of alcohol or other drug abuse. However, the instrument identified, Youth Self-Esteem Assessment, may not measure attitude towards school. The instrument needs to be aligned with the services offered, not the "big picture" desired result.

A school district implements a Service Learning program for middle school students. The project director calls the National Clearinghouse on Service Learning. The project director requests an instrument to measure his program. The clearinghouse sends the project director a handful of instruments to use as samples so that the project director can get an idea of the resources available. The project director, without a thorough review of the instruments, chooses one to use for his evaluation.

Caution: The project director did not review the questions in the instrument. The content/skill areas in the instrument may not be in alignment with what is being offered in this Service Learning program. Outcomes results of this evaluation may result in negative outcomes, even though the services provided may have been exemplary.

BOX 5.4 **CHOOSING INSTRUMENTS OFF-THE-SHELF**

- Select instruments intended to measure activities similar to your program activities.
- Make sure that the instrument has some successful history of being used with people similar to your beneficiaries. Consider factors such as beneficiary age, gender, language, and culture.
- Be sure that the instrument will provide the information you need (e.g., if your standard of success says, "80% of youth will increase their reading rates by 5 words per minute," the instrument you select should measure in words per minute).
- Some off-the-shelf instruments are administered at specific times or points in the program (e.g., standardized tests that are given only once per year). Be sure administration times work for your program.
- Some off-the-shelf instruments are intended for diagnostic purposes or large group use only. Make sure the instrument you choose is intended to demonstrate outcomes for your beneficiaries.

Source: From "Choosing Instruments Off-the-Shelf," Aguirre International, Project STAR, 1998. Produced for the Corporation for National Service, Washington, DC, 20525. Used with permission.

- The training required to administer the instrument
- The qualifications of the person administering the instrument
- A description regarding how the instrument should be administered
- Information about scoring or compiling data collected (Aguirre, 1998(a)).

Also keep in mind that the alteration or deletion of questions may affect the validity or reliability of the instrument.

How to Develop the Instruments

What do program staffs do if they cannot find an existing instrument to measure the services they are providing as indicated in their evaluation plan? The evaluation plan may identify unique indicators to be collected, describe a unique service-delivery approach to a specialized group of beneficiaries, or require the evaluation to be completed within a timeline that would not give the program time to affect the recipients of services as expected from measurements of an existing instrument.

When using the empowerment approach, program staffs are able to use the evaluation results for program improvement. Therefore, the data collected should benefit the program and may also benefit other stakeholders. If other stakeholders can use the evaluation results, this provides added value in conducting the empowerment evaluation. In reality, most nonprofit agencies develop their own data collection instruments. This allows them to tailor the instruments to meet the unique program characteristics, service indicators, as well as time and other logisitical demands.

Forming the Questions

The evaluation plan (see chapter 4) is the reference point that will provide the direction for developing the questions or framework for how the instrument needs to be developed. The plan will identify the information needed, the type of method to use, and the questions to construct.

To identify the information needed, review the evaluation plan and refer to the desired result and indicators elements. Think about the information that will demonstrate the progress towards the desired result. Will this information align with the indicators stated in the plan? To begin this process, think about the following questions: is the information needed already collected or in existing records; does the instrument need to measure knowledge, attitudes, or behavior; or does the instrument need to collect information about the opinion of participants or an observant?

When choosing the type of method, the evaluation plan will again provide information that guides the direction for this step. The evaluation plan will describe how data will be collected and who will complete the instrument. For example, the plan may state youth will complete a conflict resolution survey of an after-school program; the survey is the method, and the youth are the persons who will complete the instrument. Make sure the instrument being developed will, in fact, be usable. Will the persons for which the instrument is intended be willing to, or able to, complete the instrument? Does the instrument place unrealistic burdens on the persons administering the instrument? Is the instrument identified in the evaluation plan the method that will provide the most direct measures that will demonstrate the program's impact? Box 5.5 provides guidelines to choose the method of measurement.

After identifying the information needed and the type of method to be used, the next step in developing an instrument is to create the questions. There are two basic types of questions to consider, selection questions and supply questions.

Selection questions limit the range of choices that the respondent can choose. This allows the developer of the instrument to have control over the type of answers generated ensures that

BOX 5.5   DETERMINING THE METHOD TO MOST DIRECTLY MEASURE CHANGE

As you consider what you want to change, think about the following questions:	More Direct Measures	Less Direct Measures
Do you want to change knowledge?	• Tests • Skill assessments • Rubrics • Skill observations • Subject specific grades	• Self-report of knowledge gained (from survey, interview, journals) • Other's report of knowledge gained
Do you want to change affect, attitudes, or opinions?	• Self Report of changed attitudes (from survey, interview, journal, focus groups) • Psychological and attitudinal assessment scales	• Other's report of changed attitudes • Observation records • Portfolio inventory
Do you want to change behavior?	• Observations • Records (from attendance, achievement tests, crime)	• Self report of changed behavior (from survey, interview, journal, focus groups) • Other's report of changed behavior • Self-report of changed attitides toward behavior (from survey, interview, journal, focus groups)

Source: From "Toolkit: A User's Guide to Evaluation for National Service Programs," Aguirre International, Project STAR, 1998. Produced for the Corporation for National Service, Washington, DC, 20525. Used with permission.

the information needed will be received, and provides a format that can quickly collect and analyze the information. Examples of selection questions are mostly closed-ended questions that include yes-no responses, rating scales, checklists, categories, multiple-choice questions, and true-false responses. Supply questions do not have answer categories. They are mostly open-ended questions that allow the respondent the flexibility to answer questions using their own words. These type of questions allow respondents to provide answers that are descriptive or provides the opportunity for respondent to explain their responses. These questions also allow the respondents to share anecdotes or "great stories." Examples of supply questions include short answer questions that solicit specific information (Covert 1977).

Layout Design

When developing an instrument, the layout design is as critical as the questions and information collecting elements. The layout design needs to be user-friendly; otherwise, the participants may not bother to use the form, may not complete it accurately or correctly, or may not provide all of the information requested. There are six areas to consider when developing an instrument: instrument title, introductory statement, directions, demographics, questions, and format.

The first three areas provide the participant with information on the what, why, and how of the instrument. The title serves to identify the program and the type of service under evaluation. It also indicates the type of method to be used. The title should reference what was indicated on the evaluation plan. The introductory statement describes the instrument's purpose, how the data will be used, and information about the level of confidentiality and other ethical considerations that will be practiced. The directions provide information how to complete the instrument. These instructions should be clear and direct, yet short and simple. Participants of the instrument should not have to question how to use the instrument. If the instrument consists of more then one section that requires different instructions to complete, make sure the instructions appear before each appropriate section.

The fourth area, demographics, collects information about the evaluation participant as well as the person completing the instrument (e.g., teacher's name, observer's name). Other information related to the participant may also be needed; for example, age, gender, the place where the activity occurs, the dates of participation, and the date when the instrument has been completed. Make sure the information needed is requested; if information needed is not collected at this time, staff may have to spend time and energy to go back and get the information. In some cases, it may not be appropriate to go back to get this information, or may not be possible to get this information at a later time. However, do not ask for information that is not appropriate or needed. For example, if the survey instructions state that the respondent will remain anonymous, requesting the name of the respondent should not occur.

The fifth area, the questions, requests the information needed for the evaluation. This is the main purpose why this instrument is administered—-to gather information about the services being delivered. As described previously, program staff need to select what questions to ask and how to ask them. There are a few common guiding principles to follow when forming the questions to ask. Use language that the respondents can understand. The age, academic level, and culture need to be considered. The community may consist of respondents whose first language is other than English; therefore, the survey may need to be in both English and the community's primary language. Avoid "double-barreled" questions, questions that include two or more issue points, but asked to respond only once. Avoid using words that can bias or send a value message, encouraging a response that leans toward a specific response. When asking open-ended questions, provide enough space for the respondent to write their responses. Ask questions that have a purpose; asking questions that definitely will not be used for the evaluation is extra effort not required.

The last area to consider when developing an instrument is the format on how the instrument will be designed. The instrument needs to be pleasing to the eye and easy to follow. Program staff may want to use graphics for identifiers or for clarification of response. Make sure the font is clear, legible, and large enough for the respondent. Allow appropriate space between instructions, questions, and responses. Too much space can be as confusing as too little space. One of the common faults is trying to make the information fit on one or two pages. They tend to crowd the information, making the instrument hard to follow; and in some cases, reduce the font size so that it becomes difficult to read. It is better to have more pages or reduce the desired information, rather than cramming information into the instrument. Lastly, program staff may want to document in a footer or header the name of the program or organization that developed the instrument, the date of each new version, and other identifiers that may be needed for future use or revisions. Box 5.6 is an example of a design for a one-page survey.

Pilot Testing the Instrument

After the instrument is complete, it is important to pilot test the instrument. This instrument is new and has been customized to measure specific program services. There are a number of reasons to pilot test the instrument before use. Is there difficulty understanding or completing the instrument? Does the respondent interpret questions as intended by the way the questions are formed? Are the directions clear?

The process of pilot testing the instruments can be conducted in a number of different ways. Box 5.7 on page 71 describes one method of pilot testing the instruments (Aguirre, 1998).

Validity and Reliability

When developing an instrument, the question that often is asked is, "how valid and reliable is the instrument?" Lets first review the definitions of validity and reliability.

Validity is that the instrument actually measures the variables it was designed to measure (Rubin & Babbie, 1997; Royse & Thyer, 1997).

Reliability is whether an instrument always gets the same results when repeated under similar conditions.

For example, when using a ruler to measure length, the validity of this instrument (i.e., distance) is high because the ruler is divided in feet and inches, the increments of length. The ruler however is not a valid instrument to measure weight. The reliability of using a ruler to measure length is also very high because the results of measurement will show that a foot will always be a foot, and an inch will always be an inch. A wooden and well-constructed ruler will yield a consistent and reliable measurement time after time. If a rubber band is used as a ruler, then it will have reliability problems. An inch could become a foot if stretched.

As can be seen, these are important features in the development of an instrument. To the extent that it's possible, validity and the reliability of a developed instrument need to be kept in mind. However, is it realistic to expect program staff, having little experience in program evaluation, to develop instruments with high validity and reliability? This may be, again, a good time to revisit the empowerment evaluation approach. The purpose of the empowerment evaluation approach is to obtain information that can be used by program staff for program improvement and development. Therefore, the question program staff needs to keep in mind when developing customized instruments is, "To what extent does the instrument need to be valid and reliable so that the information received will be useful for program improvement?" Also, a second question program staff need to ask is, "as a program person, how far can I go to verify that the instrument is valid and reliable?" There may be situations where program staff may not be able to determine the validity and reliability of the instrument developed; however, the program staffs feel the information obtained from this evaluation instrument can provide them with important information that can be used for program improvement.

This chapter is not a chapter on instrumentation. However, basic validity and reliability of an instrument can be developed. Program staff can help establish the basic face of content validity of their instruments. For many researchers, face validity is the very elementary form of content validity.

Face Validity

Face validity is a form of validity determind by whether, on the face of it, a measure seems to make sense (Vogt, 1993). "Having face validity does not mean that a measure really measures what the research intends to measure; it only means that it appears to measure what the researcher intends to measure" (Rubin & Babbie, 1997, p. 178). Face validity asks the question of "Does it look right?" The best judges are the people who have knowledge of what "it" (i.e., the instrument and its items) is supposed to look like. Some of these judges are the people and sources that have particular knowledge about the subject matter. They may also come in the

---

BOX

5.6   SCHOOL READINESS SURVEY (BAY AREA TUTORS, SAN FRANCISCO)

This is a: ❑ pre-test   ❑ post-test

Dear Tutor:

This instrument will help measure school readiness and listening skills for students participating in the Bay Area Tutors Reading program. All data will remain confidential and results will be reported anonymously.

Please indicate above if this is a pre- or post-test. The pre-test should be conducted within the 1st month of the program and the post-test conducted after the students have participated in the program for at least 7 months.

Your Name: _____   Date: _____

School: _____   Students Name: _____

School Readiness

Directions: Please check ☑ all items that you observe for each student.

1. Before tutoring session begins:

❑ Student is prepared for tutoring session (e.g., read assigned material, completed homework).

❑ Student has materials (e.g., pencils, paper).

❑ Student arrives on time.

2. During tutoring session:

❑ Student follows ground rules.

❑ Student participates in tutoring session activities (e.g., participates in discussions/ answers questions).

❑ Student asks for assistance when needed.

Listening Skills

Directions: Based on your observations, please check ☑ the items that best describes your perception of this student.

❑ Student pays attention to whoever is speaking.

❑ Student does not interrupt whoever is speaking.

❑ Student actively listens and really tries to answer questions.

❑ Student is able to clearly reiterate back what the speaker said.

❑ Student demonstrates the ability of recognizing the main idea of discussions.

Thank you. Please return the completed form to the Program Manager.

Source: Developed by STAR for Aguirre International and Bay Area Tutors, San Francisco, CA. January 2002. version 2. Used with permission.

---

form of published articles and books. After a draft instrument is developed based on literature reviews, a representation of these "knowledgeable" people will examine the instrument. Afterward, they respond individually or through group discussions on the intent of the instrument and whether the instrument makes sense.

Content Validity

Content validity is a measure whose items accurately and fully represent the thing being measured. It is a matter of expert judgment (Vogt, 1993). Rubin and Babbie (1997) assert that "content validity refers to the degree to which a measure covers the range of meanings included within the concept" (p. 178). They further indicate that content validity can be established through the "researchers or other experts mak[ing] judgment about whether the measure covers the universe of facets that make up the concept" (p. 178). Through further

BOX
5.7

PILOT-TESTING GUIDELINES

1. Find participants (4–5 people) from the group of people whom you will actually be surveying or interviewing.

2. Arrange for these participants to test the pilot instrument in the conditions as close to the actual administration conditions as possible. Consider the time of day, the location, and even the method. If it is a phone interview, practice over the phone. If it is a mail survey, make sure they complete the form without any assistance, or even mail it to them. It is a good idea to record the time it takes your participant to complete the survey, especially if written.

3. After each participant completes the instrument, arrange a time to discuss the experience. This will usually last two or three times longer than it took to complete the instrument. The following are some questions you might want to ask.

Overall Questions	Individual Questions	Logistical Questions
What do you think this survey is about?	Do you think participants will understand how to answer the questions?	Are the directions clear?
What problems, if any, did you have completing the survey?	Is there language in the survey that people you know might not understand?	Were the directions clear on how to return the survey?
How do you think the information will be used?	Do you think participants will find any of these questions too sensitive?	How long did it take to complete the survey?

4. Collect the completed instruments. Read through the responses. Did participants interpret the questions the way you intended? Try to analyze and present the results of the pilot test the way you will for your actual survey or interview.

5. Share the results of your pilot test with other people who will be using the data. Does this instrument provide the data to answer their questions? Modify your instrument based on the information you have gathered.

Source: From "Toolkit: A User's Guide to Evaluation for National Service Programs," Aguirre International, Project STAR, 1998. Produced for the Corporation for National Service, Washington, DC, 20525. Used with permission.

empirical testing, the instrument will be assessed whether the measure "indeed measures what it intends to measure" (p. 179).

Both face validity and content validity are not sufficient to establish the true validity of the instrument. There are other more advanced forms of validity, i.e., criterion validity, concurrent validity, and construct validity. They however require more advanced knowledge and techniques to have them assessed and established.

Test-Retest Reliability

There are two basic types of reliability that concern program evaluation: test-retest reliability and interrater reliability.

Test-retest reliability is the correlation between scores on two administrations of the same test given to the same subjects. A high correlation indicates high reliability (Vogt, 1993). To test for test-retest reliability, ask a group of people for which that instrument was intended, to take the survey. After a period of time, ask the same group of people take the same survey a second time. Compare the results of the two administrations by individual. If the correlation between results is high, the reliability of the instrument tests out as high. An important element to consider when using test-retest reliability is the determination when it's appropriate to administer the instrument a second time. Retesting too soon can skew the correlation between results because the individual may remember how he answered the test the first time. However, waiting too long before re-testing can also skew the correlation between results because the individual may gain familiarity in the area being tested if exposed to the elements being measured.

Interrater Reliability

Interrater reliability is the extent to which raters judge occurrences in the same way; when there is agreement among raters (Vogt, 1993). To test for interrater reliability, ask a small group of people who have similar attitude or knowledge abilities to complete the instrument. Compare the results to determine the correlation between scores of the individuals. The extent to which these persons of similar ability use an instrument resulting in similar ends will indicate the instrument is reliable.

Resources for Developing Instruments

There are a number of resources that staff can research to assist them. Certainly, the library and the World Wide Web are good starting points. They could also call up professional staff evaluation consultants, as well as the funding sources for assistance. Another good source is other agencies which provide similar services.

At the end of this chapter are examples of instruments developed for community service programs as part of Aguirre International's Project STAR project. Evaluation plans are matched with the instruments to provide the reader with examples of how the relationship between the two, as described in this chapter, support and are in alignment with one another.

Strategies to Collect Data

Planning for data collection strategies and the identification of instruments mostly occur simultaneously. Before the instrument can be identified or developed, the type of information needed and the source of where that information will be obtained needs to be decided first. These decisions are part of the data collection strategy. If the data collection strategy is changed, the type of instrument to be used may need to change. Both the identified instrument and the data collection strategy need to be aligned. Therefore, even though the first part of this chapter describes how to identify or develop an instrument, followed by describing how to strategize for data collection, this is not necessarily the order of conducting these two steps. Program staffs need to find what works and what does not work as they work through these two steps simultaneously. Box 5.8 demonstrates the needs for aligning the instrument with data collection strategies.

As demonstrated in Box 5.8, data collection is the process of gathering information in a uniform and predetermined manner for future aggregation and analysis. The data collection process includes making arrangements to successfully collect the information needed for the evaluation, using identified or developed instruments appropriately, and collecting the data in a

---

BOX
5.8   **ALIGNING YOUR INSTRUMENT WITH YOUR DATA COLLECTION STRATEGY**

Program staff of an after-school literacy tutoring program at an elementary school decided, as their data collection strategy, to measure outcomes of their program by requesting each teacher to complete a one page survey of the progress students have been making in reading, including the students' latest reading test scores, each quarter. The survey, developed by program staff, was designed so that teachers had to complete a survey for each student participating in their program. However, after pilot-testing the instrument with a handful of teachers and discussing their data collecting strategy with them, program staff found that the response rate of teachers completing the instrument would be low, partly because many of the teachers had ten or more students participating in the after-school literacy program, requiring them to complete ten or more surveys, one for each student, quarterly. The burden placed on teachers would be high, and because the teachers were already inundated with other state and district mandated literacy recording requirements, the priority of completing an additional measurement would be low.

Program staff revisited their data collection strategy, and rather than requesting teachers to complete a survey, decided to have tutors administer literacy assessment instruments that could be purchased inexpensively and would do a good job measuring student progress. The reading specialist at the school agreed to provide training with the tutors and program staff on administering the assessment. Because program staff provided the support and supervision of the tutors, they were able to obtain a 95% completion of student literacy assessments. Unexpectedly, program staff found that when training the tutors how to administer the assessment instruments, the training indirectly provided a learning experience for tutors on becoming more proficient in literacy tutoring techniques.

---

timely manner. Five critical steps are required for a successful data collection process to occur: determining the type of data to be collected and from where this information will come, identifying who will be collecting the data, developing a data collection schedule, pilot testing the data collection process, and training the data collectors.

Type of Data to Be Collected

The type of data to be collected needs to reflect the indicators and desired result stated in the evaluation plan. Therefore, let's review again the evaluation plan so that the data collection strategy will align with the evaluation process. A critical part of the alignment is the type of instruments to use in collecting the data. Program staff may want to brainstorm the various types of data that reflect the indicators stated in the evaluation plan and that are in alignment with the desired result. Choose the data to be collected that will make a solid argument that the services provided did in fact contribute to the gains or change of the participants. As program staff review the list of data that can demonstrate outcome results, they may find the data that would make the most powerful statement that outcome results have been reached is not collectable. The data may not be available in the grouping or format needed, the data may be too difficult to collect, the data may not be accessible to program staff, or timing when the data would be available to program staff may not meet the timelines when program staff need the data for reporting purposes. Therefore, program staff may need to accept their second-choice data that may not make as powerful a statement as the first choice, but can be collected. Consider the following issues when deciding the type of data to collect.

From where will the information come? Will the recipients receiving the service, provide the information needed? Will the persons providing the service supply the information? Is the information already being collected; if so, where is it; who can release the information and how can the information be accessed? When should the data be collected? These are critical questions when determining the data collection strategy. In some cases, the type of instrument determines where the information will come; the type of data to be collected will be a factor as to where to go for the information. As can be seen by these questions, planning for data collection and determining the type of instruments to use must be a joint effort. It is important to emphasize the question, "can I get the information needed to determine if the services provided have generated the expected outcomes."

Identifying Who Is to Collect the Data

Collecting the data can occur at different times of the program year, depending on how the data collection strategy was designed—one time at the end of the program year, once at the beginning of the program year and once at the end of the program year, periodically between the beginning and end of the program year (e.g., quarterly, semiannually), or regularly throughout the term of the program year (e.g., weekly, monthly). If program staff are responsible for collecting the data, this task requires the staff to shift from regular program duties to conducting the data collection, a task that is very different from providing program services. Therefore, it is very easy for program staff to forget, or put off, the collection of data and miss the scheduled data collection timelines. This can be detrimental to the evaluation process. A thorough discussion of data collection schedules will be discussed later in this chapter. To reduce the possibility of missed timelines of when to collect the data, it is important to identify a person that will be responsible for monitoring the timeline and ensuring that the data is to be collected in a timely manner. This person does not necessarily need to be the person who collects the data; however, this person must be responsible for seeing that the data are collected when scheduled to do so.

When developing evaluation plans, the person responsible for seeing the data is to be collected, or minimally the position title of the person should already have been identified. If a position title is listed in the evaluation plan and not a specific person, the program director should identify a person responsible soon after the program year begins. If data needs to be collected at the beginning of the year but no one is monitoring the process, the data may not be collected at the appropriate time.

Developing a Data Collection Schedule

When identifying the type of data to collect, where the data will be obtained, and what instrument to use, the timeline as to when the data should be collected will emerge. However, if a data collection schedule is not developed and clearly lays out the timeline when the instruments should be used, there may be a tendency to forget to collect the data in a timely manner. If the data is not collected at the appropriate time, the opportunity to collect a specific data set may be missed, or if the data can still be collected, it may not measure accurately the total impact of what the program accomplished. For example, if students needed to complete a survey toward the end of a school year but school ended before filling out the survey, it will be nearly impossible to request students to complete the survey after school was out (e.g., students may not be reachable during the summer or next school year). Also, missing the opportunity to collect baseline data at the beginning of a program year can also make a big difference in the outcome results. For example, if a presurvey to measure the increase in student reading abilities was conducted late and done so after the first school quarter, the data collected would not reflect the first quarter gains that students achieved due to the services already provided.

The person responsible for collecting the data should make sure that the schedule is up-to-date and that all responsible people collecting the data have a copy. A basic data collection schedule should list the names of the instruments to be used, specific objective or program that the instrument is measuring, and the dates when the instrument should be used.

Pilot Testing the Data Collection Process

After identifying the instrument to be used, who will complete the instrument, when the instrument will be completed, and who will be responsible for the data collection process, it is important to pilot test the data collection process. The purpose of this test is to identify and eliminate problems that might not have been anticipated. Make the data collection exercise as realistic as possible. When elements of the test cannot be realistic, for example possibly the timing of the data collection process, check with those who will be involved during the real time of the data collection process and discuss the strategy. If preexisting data will be collected, conduct a dry run and make sure that the data that is needed can actually be collected. Develop relationships with the people who will be assisting or providing consent to collect the data when the time comes for data collection.

Training for the Data Collectors

The last part of the data collection strategy is to make sure the people who will be administering the instrument are trained how to do so. This will ensure that the data is collected in a consistent manner and accurately. If surveys are the instruments identified, the persons who will administer the surveys need to be trained; if program staff will be using an observation checklist, they will need to be trained; if site coordinators will be using a documentation roster to collect existing or secondary data, they need to go through the process of contacting the appropriate people to get the data and transfer the data to the roster; if programs will be using a simple log, they need to try using the log. Regardless of how simple the instrument may seem, the data collectors need to be trained, walking through the collection process and using the instruments that have been identified.

There are a few basic points to remember when training data collectors. These points (as displayed in Box 5.9) will help ensure the proper collection of useful evaluation data.

Using the Tools and Collecting the Data

Revisit the evaluation plan, the instruments identified or developed, and the data collection strategy to determine that all three areas are in alignment. Up to this point, the evaluation effort has been a planning and development phase. The next phase is to actually implement the evaluation. Therefore, this is a critical juncture before moving on. After the collection of data is complete, the last two phases will take place: the analysis of the data and the reporting of the results.

Box 5.10, 5.11, and 5.12 on pages 78–85 are three sets of evaluation plans and their associated instruments. They represent how data collection strategies and their instruments actualize the respective evaluation plan.

> **BOX**
> **5.9** POINTS TO REMEMBER FOR TRAINING DATA COLLECTORS

- Walk through the instrument with your data collectors to point out specific instructions.
- Provide an example of a completed instrument or interview transcript for your data collectors.
- Provide clear instructions and/or a script (for phone surveys or interviews) for your data collectors to follow.
- Allow your data collectors to practice with a "standard" data set or example to make sure everyone is getting the same answers, when consistency is desirable. Allow interviewers and focus group facilitators to practice in a "role play."

Summary

All too often, program staff are quick to find a tool for data collection before taking the time to determine what information is needed and how the information will be obtained. This chapter discusses the data collection strategies and identification of instruments that will measure the desired results from services delivered. Special considerations need to be addressed around data collection strategies and instrument identification when using the empowerment evaluation approach. Because program staff contribute to the selection of instruments, data collection process, and analysis of the data collected, the instruments identified and data collection methods used need to be basic and place minimal burden on staff.

References

Aguirre International, Project STAR (1998a). *Choosing instruments off-the-shelf.* Produced for the Corporation for National Service, Washington, DC, 20525.

Aguirre International, Project STAR (1998b). *Toolkit: A user's guide to evaluation for national service programs.* Washington, DC: The Corporation for National Service.

Corcoran, K., & Fischer, J. (1999a). *Measures for clinical practice: A source book: Vol. 1. Couples, families, and children* (3rd ed.). New York: Free Press.

Corcoran, K., & Fischer, J. (1999b). *Measures for clinical practice: A source book: Vol. 2. Adults* (3rd ed.). New York: Free Press.

Covert, Robert W. (1977). *Guidelines and criteria for constructing questionaires.* Charlottesville: University of Virginia, Evaluation Research Center, Curry School of Education.

Gabor, P., Unrau, Y., Grinnell, Jr., R. (1998). *Evaluation for social workers: A quality improvement approach for the social services* (2nd ed.). Boston: Allyn and Bacon.

Neeting, F. E., Kettner, P. M., & McMurtry, S. L. (1993). *Social work macro practice.* New York: Longman.

Nugent, W. R., Sieppert, J. D., & Hudson, W. W. (2001). *Practice evaluation for the 21st century.* Belmont, CA: Brooks/Cole.

Nurius, P. L., & Hudson, W. W. (1993). *Human services: Practice, evaluation, and computers: A practical guide for today and tomorrow.* Pacific Grove, CA: Brooks/Cole.

Royse, D., & Thyer, B. (1997). *Program evaluation: An introduction* (2nd ed.). Chicago: Nelson-Hall.

Rubin, A., & Babbie, E. (1997). *Research methods for the social worker* (3rd ed.). Pacific Grove, CA: Brooks/Cole.

Sax, G. (1989). *Principals of educational and psychological measurement and evaluation* (3rd ed.). Belmont, CA: Wadsworth. University of Washington.

United States General Accounting Office (1993). *Developing and using questionnaires* (GAO/PEMD-10.1.7). Washington, DC: Author.

Vogt, W. P. (1993). *Dictionary of statistics and methodology.* Newbury Park, CA: Sage).

BOX 5.10

SAMPLE EVALUATION PLAN AND INSTRUMENT (COMMUNITY SERVICE EVALUATION PLAN)

Community Service Evaluation Plan

Your Name: J. Smith   Date: July 2001

Program/activity: Community Service Development Initiative   Site Location: County

Activity Start Date: 9/1/01   End Date: 8/30/02   Report Due Date: 9/30/02

1. **Describe the Activity.** Describe who will be providing and participating in the activity, what the activity will be, when the activity will happen, for how long and where the activity will take place, etc.).	Each of 20 VISTA Volunteers will be placed in twenty communities in the state of XX for one year to assist community organizations, neighborhood groups, or local governments develop or expand existing services that meet the needs of youth as described in the America Promise Initiative.
2. **Describe the beneficiaries.** Briefly describe the people your activity will serve (participants' ages or grade levels, and/or special characteristics).	Community organizations, neighborhood groups, and local governments will benefit directly; the people these organizations serve will benefit indirectly.
3. **Describe anticipated output.** Briefly describe the number of participants you hope to serve, average daily attendance if applicable, and/or amount of time you hope participants spend in the program.	The development of new services to meet a need in the community or the expansion of existing services to reach more people in the community.
4. **Describe desired participant outcome.** Write what you hope to see (changed or added to) in your beneficiaries because of this activity.	Programs developed or expanded will meet community needs and will provide quality services.
5. **Describe indicators.** List items that are concrete and observable that you will look at to determine whether you achieve your desired participant outcome.	Tasks that are important for the delivery of quality community program services will be conducted.

6. **Describe data collection method and instrument(s).** Identify instrument(s) (i.e., pre/post surveys, observation log, grade sheets, etc.). Describe who will complete each instrument, when, and who will collect data. Include any other important data collection information.

Instrument(s) title?	Who will complete?	When?	Who will collect data?
Community Organization Representative Survey	Director or Coordinator of the project.	The Survey will be completed twice, once at the beginning of the program development year and a second time at the end of the year.	Project Director

Additional data collection notes: _____

_____

7. **Describe anticipated outcome result.** Write how you plan to determine the degree to which your program has been successful in achieving your desired participant outcome.	80% of the community organizations, neighborhood groups, or local government will have moved forward toward developing or expanding community services.
8. **Identify who will:** Oversee the evaluation process. Tally the data. Analyze the data. Report results.	Project Director Project Director _____ Project Director _____ Project Director _____ _____

(continued)

AmeriCorps*VISTA Program
Community Organization/Representative Survey

Community Organization/Representative:

This survey measures the outcomes of the efforts made by the AmeriCorps*VISTA volunteers during this program year. This information will be placed in an annual report for the Corporation for National Service. Please complete this survey and return it to your AmeriCorps*VISTA representative. Thank you.

Name of Community: _____   Date: _____

Person Completing Survey: _____ Organization/Group: _____

Community Organization/Representative:

Parks and Recreation: _____   Community Center: _____   School: _____

Community Leader: _____   Concerned Citizen(s): _____   Other: _____

I. What *primary* program development/improvement effort are you hoping to achieve in your community during your participation in the AmeriCorps*VISTA project?

[ ] Implement New Program   [ ] Expand Existing Program   [ ] Increasing the Quality of
                                                                           Program

Did you complete a New Program Profile? [   ] Yes   [   ] No (if not, please contact your
                                                              supervisor to complete a profile)

If implementing a new program, where in the continuum of program development is your community at:

Please check one response for each of the following tasks:

Program Development Tasks	Not Yet Begun	Less Than Half	More Than Half	Completed	Not Applicable
Educate the Community					
Action Group					
Plan Goals and Timelines					
Develop Partnerships					
Needs Assessments					
Community Resource Mapping					
Program Philosophy and Goals					
Program Structure Developed					
Program Evaluation Developed					
Incorporation					
Board of Directors					
By-Laws Created					
Staffing					
Creation of Handbooks and Other					
Public Relations/Marketing					

Comments:

If Expanding an Existing Program:

Please check one response to each task:

Program Development Tasks	Not Yet Begun	Less Than Half	More Than Half	Completed	Not Applicable
Educate the Community					
Needs Assessment					
Staffing					
Community Resource Mapping					
Evaluation					
Public Relations/Marketing					

Comments:

If Increasing the Quality of Program Services:

Please check open response to each task:

Program Development Tasks	Not Yet Begun	Less Than Half	More Than Half	Completed	Not Applicable
Educate the Community					
Assess Program Needs					
Create a Training Plan					
Provide Appropriate Trainings					
Organize School Age Connections Meetings					
Accreditation					
Research/Provide Resources					

Comments:

II. In addition to your primary effort of program development, program expansion, or increasing the quality of your program, are you increasing the Capacity/Sustainability of your Organization?

[ ] Yes   [ ] No

If Increasing the Capacity/Sustainability of Organization:

Please check one response to each task:

Program Development Tasks	Not Yet Begun	Less Than Half	More Than Half	Completed	Not Applicable
Complete Program Funding Needs Form					
Identify Funding Sources					
Assist in Grant Writing					
Develop Fundraising/Special Event Plan					
Educate the Community					

Comments:

Overall, to what extent did you reach your expectations this program year in reaching the results you intended?

_____Not at all   _____A little   _____Some   _____Most/All

Other Comments:

BOX

5.11   SAMPLE EVALUATION PLAN AND INSTRUMENT (VOLUNTEER SERVICES EVALUATION PLAN)

Your Name: J. Smith   Date: 2/12/01
Program Name: Foster Grandparent Program   Site Location: County
Activity Start Date: 9/1/00   End Date: 6/10/01   Report Due Date: 8/15/01
Objective Title: Voluneteer Assignment Descriptions

1. **Activity** Describe the national service activity you will be evaluating. (Describe the who, what, when, and where—the delivery structure you use to make your outcomes happen.)	Teachers and school administrators at 20 Head Start, pre-school, and elementary school programs will complete a Volunteer Assignment Description (VAD) for each of 300 pre- and elementary school students who will receive tutoring (one-on-one and small group) from up to 51 FGP volunteers, each FGP volunteer meeting with each student daily (4-5 times per week depending on the station schedule) for the entire school year, as measured by accurate completion of the PFI elements listed in the VAD.
2. **Beneficiaries** Briefly describe the people (and estimate the number) your activity will serve.	300 pre- and elementary school students will bene-fit; each student has a disability or special need (physical, educational, emotional).
3. **Desired Result** Explain what change will occur because of the described activity.	Accurate VADs to provide direction for the FGP volunteers to effectively provide tutoring services to students.
4. **Indicators** Describe the concrete, observable things you will look at to see whether you are making progress toward your desired result.	Descriptions of the needs (e.g., disability), type of activities to be performed, accomplishments to be completed and realistic impacts correctly stated.
5. **Method/Title of Measure** Describe the method you will use to determine if the described change occurs. Include the title of your instrument (e.g., Teacher Opinion Survey).	a. The VADs will be completed by the beginning of October and reviewed. b. VAD Follow-up Form will be completed in May.
6. **Standard of Success** Define a level of success you hope to achieve.	a. 80% of the teachers/administrators will have completed at least 3 of the 4 PFI elements listed on the VAD with a rating of 4 or 5. (Anticipated Impacts must be one of the 3 accurately completed.) b. Of those VADs that were accurately completed, 85% of the students will have achieved the desired anticipated impacts as reported on the VAD Follow-up Form.
7. **Respondents/Number of Measurements** Describe who will complete each instrument (include an estimate of the number). When measures do not include respondents, e.g., water quality tests, include an estimate of the number and frequency of measures to be taken.	a. 100 teachers and administrators will complete a VAD for each of the students when students begin participation in the FGP tutoring program. b. 100 teachers and administrators will complete the VAD Follow-up Forms in May.

8. **Data Collection** Describe who will be collecting the data and how often data will be collected.	a. The Volunteer Coordinator will collect copies of the VADs from teachers in October as well as when new students begin participation in the FGP tutoring program. b. The Volunteer Coordinator will distribute and collect the VAD Follow-up Forms in May of the following year.
9. **Data Aggregation** Describe who will be aggregating the data and how often data will be aggregated	The Advisory Council Planning Committee will check the VADs for accuracy in March-April of 2001 and at the beginning of the school year (October) and when new students begin the FGP tutoring program.
10. **Data Analysis** Describe who will be analyzing the data and how often data will be analyzed.	The Advisory Council Planning Committee will compare the VADs with the VAD Follow-up Forms in the Spring (May-June) and will report the % of teachers/administrators that accurately completed the VADs.
11. **Corporation for National Service Report** Describe who will write the report and how often the report is due.	a. The Advisory Council Planning Committee will report the % of VADs that were completed accurately in April 2001 and in October of succeeding years. b. The Advisory Council Planning Committee will report the % of VAD Follow-up Forms that are in alignment with the VADs from the previous October.
12. **Reporting Loop** Describe other forms of reporting evaluation information (newsletter, press release), who will write these reports, and how often it occurs.	a. The Advisory Council Planning Committee will report the results to the Advisory Council and program staff. b. The Project Director will report the results to the volunteers at inservice meetings. c. Project staff will share results with volunteer station staff and with other stakeholders. d. Results will be reported to United Way in January of 2002.

(continued)

BOX 5.11

Sample Evaluation Plan and Instrument (Volunteer Services Evaluation Plan) (continued)

Foster Grandparent Program
ABC County
Volunteer Assignment Description Review Guide

Grandparent's Name _____   School/Agency _____

Teacher/Supervisor _____   Child's First Name _____

Reviewer _____   Date of Review: _____

Programming for Impact Elements	Vague 1	2	Needs More Clarification 3	4	Clear 5
Need Detailed information of the issue to be addressed and the current status of the student. *Ken reads below grade level; his STAR score in the Fall was 1.5.*	Little detail and lacks status of student.		Describes need; however, lacks status of student.		Detailed and list status of student.
Activities The activities address the need; the type of service proposed is realistic. *FGP will meet individually during the school day with Ken to read a variety of material and work on comprehension of material read.*	Activity is vague and not realistic.		Describes type of activity; however, service expectations are only somewhat realistic.		Describes type of activity and service expectations are realistic.
Anticipated Accomplishments Ability to identify and count the effort to be performed: what will be done, how long, how often. *FGP will provide tutoring for 30 minutes per day for 186 student contact days.*	Lacks items to be counted.		Describes what will be done; lacks how long and how often.		Describes what, how long, and how often.
Anticipated Impact Aligned with the activity; a minimum level of change hoped to occur is stated. *Ken will increase his STAR reading score to at least 3.0 in the Spring.*	Not aligned; lacks minimum level of change.		Aligned with activity; lacks minimum level of change.		Aligned and describes minimum level of change.

Source: All forms in Box 5.11 were created by Project STAR. Used with permission of Aguirre International.

BOX
5.12   SAMPLE EVALUATION PLAN AND INSTRUMENT (SKILL DEVELOPMENT EVALUATION PLAN)

Web of Support Outcome: Cognitive/Intellectual   **Date:** 9/9/99
Program Name: SAMPLE-Marketable Skills-Proficiency in a trade   **Your Name:** Hank H.
Beginning Date of Program/Activity: 10/01/99   **End Date of Program/Activity:** 5/31/00

OBJECTIVES

A. What is the issue(s) concerning youth that you would like to improve? (e.g., poor academic performance, gangs)	Students need trade skills.
B. Program/Activity To address this issue: • What is the Constructive Activity or program you will be conducting? • What Caring Adult characteristics are needed for this program/activity? • What constitutes a Safe Place for this program/activity?	• The Jefferson after-school program conducts a woodworking class after school on Tuesdays and Thursdays from 3:30pm to 5:00pm throughout the school year. • Caring adults will have knowledge of wood-working and equipment and how to teach students the trade. They will be patient, kind, and flexible. • The vocational building at Jefferson High School will be the safe place. Everyone will need to wear proper equipment and observe safety rules.
C. Number of youth What is the number of youth this activity or program will serve?	Number of Youth: 45 Description of participating youth: Low income. Ages 12–16 at risk youth.
D. Desired Outcome What is the desired outcome of this activity or program?	Youth will gain a trade skill (woodworking).
E. Indicators What indicators can you use to see if this desired outcome was achieved?	• Youth will know types of woodworking equipment • Youth will know how to use/operate equipment • Youth will know how to do woodworking safely
F. Instrument What type of instrument will you use to measure the indicators of this activity or program?	Post Youth Survey Post Teacher Observation Checklist Attendance Log
G. Level of Success How will you know if you have achieved success?	85% of the 45 participating students will acquire a trade skill (woodworking). Students will have acquired woodworking skills if they move up an average of 2 points on each of pre/post teacher observations.

EVALUATION PLAN

1. Who will fill instruments out?	How many: (Complete only those which apply.) __X__ Youth? __X__ Staff? _____ Other adults?
2. How often will they be filled out and when?	(__) Beginning (__) Middle (X) End of Activity/Program Cycle Date(s): 5/00
3. Who is responsible for:	Collecting the data? Teacher Aggregating the data? Hank H. Analyzing the data? Hank H. Reporting the results? Hank H. Reporting Due Date: 7/15/00

(continued)

BOX
5.12   SAMPLE EVALUATION PLAN AND INSTRUMENT (SKILL DEVELOPMENT PLAN) (CONTINUED)

[Name of Program]
1999–2000 Vocational Technical Program
Skill in Tool Use Assessment

Child: _____   Age: _____   Gender: Female / Male

Completed by: _____   Location: _____

For each of the following items, please circle the one number from 1 (low) to 4 (high) that best describes this child's ability to use a given tool effectively (including safe operation). Please write any additional comments in the space provided or on the back of this form. Thank you!

Child's ability to use the following tools:	(Pre) Date:				(Post) Date:				Change	Comments
	Low			High	Low			High		
Hammer	1	2	3	4	1	2	3	4		
Screwdriver	1	2	3	4	1	2	3	4		
Phillips screwdriver	1	2	3	4	1	2	3	4		
Saw	1	2	3	4	1	2	3	4		
Coping saw	1	2	3	4	1	2	3	4		
Miter saw	1	2	3	4	1	2	3	4		
Level	1	2	3	4	1	2	3	4		
Tape measure	1	2	3	4	1	2	3	4		
Square	1	2	3	4	1	2	3	4		
								Total		

Additional comments: _____

_____

[Name of Program]
1999–2000 Vocational Technical Program
Individual Growth Assessment

Child: _____ Age: _____   Gender: Female / Male

Completed by: _____   Location: _____

For each of the following items, please circle the one number from 1 (low) to 4 (high) that best describes this child's ability to use a given tool effectively (including safe operation). Please write any additional comments in the space provided or on the back of this form. Thank you!

Skills:	(Pre) Date:				(Post) Date:				Change	Comments
	Low			**High**	**Low**			**High**		
Respects tools	1	2	3	4	1	2	3	4		
Understanding sequences	1	2	3	4	1	2	3	4		
Safety awareness	1	2	3	4	1	2	3	4		
Listens to directions	1	2	3	4	1	2	3	4		
Follows directions	1	2	3	4	1	2	3	4		
Tries new things	1	2	3	4	1	2	3	4		
Is a self starter	1	2	3	4	1	2	3	4		
Helps others	1	2	3	4	1	2	3	4		
Is patient	1	2	3	4	1	2	3	4		
Solves problems	1	2	3	4	1	2	3	4		
Gets along with others	1	2	3	4	1	2	3	4		
								Total		

Additional comments: _____

_____

Source: All forms in Box 5.12 were created by Project STAR. Used with permission of Aguirre International.

DATA ANALYSIS AND REPORTING

The last two steps of the evaluation process are to analyze the data collected and to report the results to stakeholders. Generally, the actual effort of conducting these two steps occurs later in the evaluation cycle (data analysis tends to be conducted in the middle of the program year and end of the year; reporting to stakeholders tend to occur after the results of the evaluation are found); however, the planning and preparation for these two steps need to occur at the beginning of the evaluation process. Without planning now, when reaching the point of analyzing the data or writing the report, the tasks might not be doable because of lack of resources, expertise, or timing. Make sure you have a reasonable time line so that the data can be analyzed in time for reporting.

Analyzing the Data

When planning for data analysis, the process includes deciding on the appropriate type of analysis to conduct, preparing for the data analysis, conducting the analysis, summarizing the results after completing the analysis, and comparing the actual results with the desired results and standards identified when the evaluation plan was developed. The analysis provides the answers to the evaluation questions first asked when the development of the evaluation began. Keep in mind that two areas need to be considered when conducting the analysis: the analysis of data from the process evaluation, which calculates the results that describe the accomplishments achieved; and the analysis of data from the outcome evaluation, which calculates the results that describe the changes that occurred because of services provided. Examples of these questions are listed in Box 6.1.

Deciding on the Appropriate Analysis to Conduct

When conducting an analysis, it can be very basic, using simple math, or it can be highly statistical. For the purposes of this book and in keeping with the empowerment evaluation approach, the analysis described in this chapter will focus on basic statistical analysis.

Data analysis begins by developing an analysis plan. This plan describes how the analysis will be conducted. The analysis plan should be developed at the same time when the evaluation plan and instruments are being developed. Because the instruments are the tools that are used to collect the data, and the data is what is being analyzed, the instruments play a major role in the development of an analysis plan. For example, if the data collection tool to be used was an existing instrument, that instrument may come with an analysis plan. However, if program staff developed their instrument, program staff will also need to develop an analysis plan specific to that instrument.

Let's consider the situation where the program staffs develop their own instruments. The first step in developing an analysis plan is to take the instrument and determine what questions

BOX
6.1

RESPONDING TO PROCESS EVALUATION AND OUTCOME EVALUATION QUESTIONS

Process Evaluation Question: Did you do what you said you were going to do?
Outcome Evaluation Question: What changed because of the services provided?

need to be analyzed. Reviewing the evaluation plan can provide direction for this task. The evaluation plan describes the desired program results. It also details the data collection and analysis processes. For example, will each individual question need to be analyzed? If so, how will each question be analyzed to determine change (e.g., calculating the rating of each question based on a rating scale)? Is the information collected quantitative or qualitative? If quantitative, what statistical analyses need to be applied? If qualitative, should a content analysis be applied or will other appropriate approaches be needed?

The second part of the evaluation plan is to determine how the standard of success it is stated. This statement will help identify the type of analysis that will need to be applied; the frequency, percent distribution, mean, change of score from baseline data to post data, or content analysis will all come into play. Program staff will either be calculating basic mathematical formulas or categorizing textual information by content area.

A tool that has assisted community service programs plan for their analysis is a table that lists questions to consider as program staff determine the type of analysis to conduct. This table (as seen in Box 6.2) provides questions of how program staff want to report their results and the type of analysis to use in response to the specific question.

Preparing for the Analysis

The analysis is conducted after the evaluation plan has been developed, instruments have been identified, and the collection of data conducted. However, before actually conducting the analysis, the data needs to be prepared for analysis.

Let's first revisit the data collected. In what form is the data? Is the data on individualized survey forms, on a summary data collection form where existing data was transferred on to a common form (e.g., number of student absences by student on one form), or in written format in response to open-ended questions? The form in which the data is available should not be a surprise, because program staff had already identified the instrument, and an analysis plan should have already been developed on how the data will be analyzed.

The next important step in preparing the data for the analysis is to "clean the data." It requires the evaluator to first verify that the forms are completely filled out, the responses to questions are clearly marked or legible, and that there are no indications that the forms were completed with little serious thought (e.g., rating scales or multiple choice questions show a single response, aswers to open-end questions are obviously juvenile). Take these instruments and place them to the side. These instruments should not be used in the analysis. They can skew the results in an untruthful manner. Do not discard these instruments, but label them as inappropriate for analysis and file them accordingly.

If using spreadsheets or a database to tabulate the data from instruments, the program analyst may need to code the data before entering it into the data system. The process of coding is

BOX
6.2 STANDARD OF SUCCESS QUESTIONS AND TYPES OF DATA ANALYSIS

While you examine your instrument, think about the following questions:	Analysis
Do you want to report the number of people who answered each question?	A count
Do you want to report how many people answered "a," "b," or "c"?	A frequency
Do you want to report what percentage of people answered "a," "b," or "c"?	A percentage distribution
Do you want to report an average score?	A mean
Do you want to report a change in score from a pretest to a posttest?	Change in scores
Do you have open-ended questions?	Content analysis

dependent on two elements: whether the data are in a form which needs to be tallied, and whether a spread sheet or database will be used in the tabulation. If both of these elements are true, then coding will be an important step in preparing for analysis. Before the spreadsheet or database is developed, the evaluator needs to determine how the questions in the instrument will be coded so that, when entering data into the system, codes can be entered rather than the actual data responses. For example, if the instrument included questions with rating scales, a rating scale number can be entered into the data system rather than words (e.g., 1 = none, 2 = a little, 3 = some, and 4 = a lot). Entering a number rather than a four- or five-letter word can save time and be less confusing when entering the data in the system.

These are a few steps that may need to be taken in preparing data for the analysis. The type of preparation and the amount of preparation of data will depend on the evaluation plan developed, the instrument identified, and the method of data collection.

Basic Statistical Analysis

Statistics refers to the numbers and the use of quantitative and mathematical procedures to summarize features of data. As a tool, statistics assist us to better describe and understand the data that we collected. Based on the statistical information developed, we can illustrate, make predictions, or apply inferences that would hopefully lead to better decision-making.

Although there are many statistics and statistical procedures with various degrees of difficulties, there are two main types of statistics: (a) descriptive statistics, and (b) inferential statistics. Descriptive statistics are used to summarize the characteristics of a sample or, if all cases were studied, of the population. Inferential statistics are procedures for determining whether it is possible to make generalizations about characteristics of the population based on data collected from a sample.

The following discussions and summaries draw mainly from Atherton and Klemmack (1982). They are intended to provide brief descriptions of some of the major statistics and their usage. Readers should consult textbooks on social statistics for more in-depth and detailed explanations and discussions. In most situations, many of the simple program evaluation projects in human services only require the use of the basic one-variable presentations or multi-variable comparisons with descriptive statistics. A few of them may go to the extent of using chi-square, Pearson's r, or t-tests. Therefore, lack of in-depth understanding, or fear of statistics should not become barriers that keep human service providers from conducting simple program evaluation. Certainly, more complicated and in-depth program evaluation may require more sophisticated research design and statistics.

Levels of Measurement

Characteristics of a phenomenon that is being studied are referred to as variables. Each variable will have a range of attributes that are called values. Values can be expressed as discrete symbols or continuous numbers. For example, program participants have many demographic characteristics that include gender, age, ethnic background, and others. Each of these variables has a different set of values or attributes. There are "male" and "female" (symbol) for gender and actual biological years (number) for age.

Based on their discrete or continuous natures, variables are identified into the four levels of measurement: nominal, ordinal, interval, and ratio. Nominal variables are the basic and simple variables that are merely naming of the objects. Groupings, categories, or listings are some of the examples. Gender as a nominal variable has two values: male or female. A nominal variable does not imply ranking and order of its values.

Variables that have order and ranking are ordinal variables. Small, medium, and large imply the order of three sizes. They do not, however, suggest the differences among its values are equal. As many readers can relate to the experience that in a fast-food restaurant, a large drink is not necessarily three times larger than the small and two times larger than the medium!

Interval level variables have meaningful and equal distance among values. Ratio variables are similar to interval variables; but a ratio variable has an absolute zero and interval variable does not. Absolute zero point means there is a true zero on the measuring scale. A drunk driver that never shows up for the court-ordered and mandatory drunk-driving class has a true zero class attendance. You can express temperature in different numeric degrees as an interval variable. In fact, the so-called zero degree does not imply there is an absence of temperature, or no temperature at all. Although there are differences between interval and ratio variables, in most research and evaluation data analyses, they are often treated as one level of measurement.

Finally, there is a hierarchy among these different levels. A ratio or interval variable can be reorganized into an ordinal or nominal level variable. For example, actual age distributions can be reorganized as older, middle, and younger groups or the 50+ group, 30–49 group, and the 30 and younger group. However, nominal variable has to stay as nominal, and ordinal as ordinal. Gender is a nominal variable that has two nominal values: female and male. It cannot become an ordinal variable, because there is no mathematical order or rank between female and male.

Descriptive Statistics

There are four major categories of descriptive statistics: frequency distribution and presentation of data, which includes frequency distributions and graphic presentation; measures of central tendency; measure of dispersion/variability; and measure of association.

I. Frequency Distribution and Presentation of Data

A. Frequency distributions

1. Frequency distributions (fd): listing of case counts per category
2. Cumulative frequency distributions (cfd): listing of added case counts
3. Percentage distributions (%): listing of proportions per category
4. Cumulative percentage distributions (c%): listing of added proportions
5. Frequency and percentage distributions: listing of both case counts and proportions

Box 6.3 describes examples of various forms and presentations of frequency distributions.

B. Graphic presentation

Bar graph: used for nominal variables to indicate frequency distribution of a variable by the height of the bars.

Histogram: used for interval and ratio level variables by the height and width of the bars.

Pie chart: used for nominal to ratio level variable by indicating segments of the whole.

Scattergram: used for interval and ratio variables by plotting data on a chart according to the horizontal axis and vertical axis. It is used to indicate the direction and strength of a correlation/association.

II. Measures of Central Tendency

These are measures that describe how data are congregated. They provide a summary and report the "typical" attributes of the data. They serve as the common denominator for comparing two sets of data.

Types:

Mean: It is the sum of all the values of a variable divided by the number of values, e.g., $(1+7+3+6+3) \div 5 = 4$. This is what most people refer to as the "average." Mean score is sensitive to extreme values. It is used for interval or ratio level data. It is also the base for many other more complicated statistics such as standard deviations and t-tests.

Mode: It tells which value(s) in the distribution of values is (are) observed more frequently than the others, the most "popular" or "often identified" value(s). For example, on a five-point scale of 1 to 5, 60 of the hundred respondents pick 4 as their answer; the mode for this item is 4. It is used for nominal or higher level data.

Median: It divides any distribution of values into two equal parts or proportions. The median is the "middle" point. It is least affected by extreme values and therefore is the most stable central tendency measure. For example, $10 is the median hourly wage for a group of 7 people who make different hourly incomes of $3, $7, $9, $10, $13, $50, and $100. The most common use of this measure is the Median Household Income. It is used for ordinal or higher level data.

Since mean, mode, and median each have their own limitations, one must consider reporting more than one measure of central tendency to provide a more comprehensive and accurate picture of the data.

DISTRIBUTIONS OF NUMBER OF PARTICIPANTS PER DAY

	fd	Cfd	%	c%
Monday	20	20	10%	10%
Tuesday	20	40	10%	20%
Wednesday	40	80	20%	40%
Thursday	40	120	20%	60%
Friday	60	180	30%	90%
Saturday	20	200	10%	100%
Total (N)	200		100%	

III. Measure of Dispersion or Variability

These are measures that describe the spread of distribution of values, and the way in which values scatter themselves around a measure of central tendency (i.e., mean, mode, or median).

Types:

Minimum: it is the lowest value of the data (i.e., the age of the youngest participant).

Maximum: it is the highest value of the data (i.e., the age of the oldest participant).

Range: it is the distance between the maximum and the minimum (i.e., the age range among participants). The formula is: (max. - min. + 1).

Interquartile range: it is the distance between the 75th percentile and the 25th percentile (75%–25%). It helps to eliminate extreme cases on both ends and focus on the core data, i.e., the values/ages of the extreme young and extreme old participants.

Variance: it is calculated as the mean of the sum of the squared differences (of the values from the arithmetic mean). Variance is the average squared deviation that tells the variation in the data. Variance is key to the development of other important measures, including standard deviation. A standard deviation is the square root of a variance.

Standard deviation: a measure of the dispersion of scores around the arithmetic mean in the original score units. The larger the standard deviation reflects the greater the spread of scores around the mean and among each other.

IV. Measurement of Association

The basic concern for the measurement of association is "how things change together?" Association and correlation are two related but different terms in this measure. Association refers to the fact that two variables are related and changed together. For example, when there are more people at the party, the more fun the party will get, and the more people will come to the party. Correlation, however, refers to more than association; it also tells the direction (positive or negative) and the strength or significance of the correlations (statistically significant or not significant). Certain measures of correlation are indicated by a score within the range of –1 to +1. Examples of common statistical measures include: chi square, Spearman's rho, Kendall's tau, and Pearson's r.

Inferential Statistics

Inferential statistics attempts to make generalizations of collected data to the general population. It involves the use of experimental designs and the use of many specialized procedures. Its applications involve hypothesis testing and the examination of statistically significant differences.

I. Hypothesis testing: it includes the development of research hypothesis and null hypothesis. The null hypotheses that are to be tested and be determined as reject or fail to reject at a certain rejection level or level of confidence.

II. Statistical significance: after the determination of the rejection level on the base of a normal curve, the evaluator may decide whether it is a one-tailed or two-tailed assessment. If the results are different from the normal happening, and this difference is happening not by chance only; then the question is whether the difference is statistically significant enough.

III. Statistically significant differences: these measures give the evaluator the sense of confidence of the data and the abilities to make generalizations.

Some of most commonly used tests include: chi square, U test, Z test, t test, F test, and ANOVA.

Box 6.4 presents a simple guide for choosing the appropriate statistics for many simple evaluation and research tasks.

An example of how the choice of evaluation design and methodology employed for data collection determines the analysis approach is demonstrated in Box 6.5.

Analyzing Qualitative Data

Qualitative data comes in the form of text. The type of questions asked to collect this data are open-ended questions, the use of journals, or other methods of data collection that allow respondents to provide information in their own words (e.g., collecting information using focus groups or interviews). In many cases, this information is used as anecdotes for reports or for "great stories" in providing examples of the success of the program. However, this information can also be processed in a systematic fashion and used as data to report outcome results.

When this information is gathered using methods that are systematically collected, and the information is categorized by common themes, general statements can be made about the program services. This information can represent generalizations of the entire program and not just examples of a couple of individuals or stories of an event. The process used to develop a system of extracting the common themes from text is called content analysis. This method of analysis categorizes the responses of individuals based on these common themes, and then takes these responses and makes general statements for each category identified. The following steps are generally followed when conducting a content analysis.

Basic Steps to Content Analysis

Identify the Unit of Analysis—The unit of analysis is the block of text that describes what is to be measured. The unit includes *who* said *what*. The *what* can be described in a paragraph, sentence, idea, or word. However, the number of units should not include so many that the general statements developed from each unit do not focus on specific outcomes that want to be

BOX
6.4   **BASIC AND FREQUENTLY USED STATISTICS**

A. One variable analysis:

1. Distribution
   Frequency distribution, percentage distribution, cumulative frequency, and cumulative percentage.
2. Measures of central tendency
   Mean, mode, and median.
3. Measures of dispersion
   Minimum, maximum, range, interquartile range, variance, and standard deviation.

B. Two or more variables analysis:

Level of Measurement	Test for significant association • To what extent are the two variables correlated?	Test for significant differences • Is the difference between groups at a significant level? • Is the difference a result of chance or a result of the independent variable?
Nominal	**Chi-square, Mean, Mode, Median, Range, Percentage** • Two nominal variables • The correlation between programs (nominal variable—graduate or undergraduate) and success in obtaining a job (nominal variable—Yes or No) • Is there a significant relationship between programs (graduate and undergraduate) that they graduated from and their success (successful or unsuccessful) in obtaining a job?	**Chi-square (χ^2)** • Two nominal variables • The difference between graduate and undergraduate (independent variable) degree holders success (dependent variable) in obtaining jobs. • Is there a significant difference between Bachelor's and Master's students in their success in obtaining a job following their completion of their studies?
Ordinal	**Spearman's Rho, Kendall's Tau** • Test for correlation (strength, direction) between two groups on an ordinal scale. • One nominal variable and one ordinal variable • Test for correlation between a group of husbands and wives (nominal variable) on an ordinal scale (nonsupportive, supportive, and very supportive) designed to measure spouse's attitudes toward each other regarding the fact that they are childless. • Is there a statistically significant correlation between gender (husband or wife) and their attitudes toward their spouses regarding the fact that they are childless?	**Mann-Whitney U test** • Test for difference between two groups on an ordinal scale. • One nominal variable and one ordinal variable • Test for difference between a group of husbands and wives (nominal variable) on an ordinal scale (nonsupportive, supportive, and very supportive) designed to measure spouse's attitudes toward each other regarding the fact that they are childless. • Is there a statistically significant difference between husbands and wives in their attitudes toward each other regarding the fact that they are childless?

(continued)

BOX
6.4 — BASIC AND FREQUENTLY USED STATISTICS *(CONTINUED)*

Ordinal *(continued)*	**Spearman's Rho, Kendall's Tau** *(continued)*	
	• Test for regression (prediction) between two ordinal scales. • To what extent clients' level of satisfaction (low, moderate, high) has correlation to clients' level of participation (low, moderate, high)? • Will clients have high level of participation also have high level of satisfaction and vice versa?	
Interval and Ratio	**Pearson's *r*** • Test for correlation between two groups on an interval/ratio scale. • One nominal variable (two groups) and one interval/ratio variable (a scale) • Is there a significant correlation between students' hours of study and their test score for the course?	***t* tests, *Z* test, *F* test** • One nominal variable and one interval/ratio variable. • Test for significant difference between two groups on an interval/ratio scale. • Is there a significant difference between 1st year graduate students and senior Bachelor's students (nominal variable) on their IQ scores? **ANOVA** (Analysis of variance, "extended t-test") • One nominal variable and one interval/ratio variable. • Test for statistically significant difference between two or more groups on an interval/ratio variable. • Is there a significant difference among bachelor, graduate and doctoral students (nominal) on their IQ scores (interval/ratio)?

emphasized. These units of analysis are the category descriptions that the evaluator, who analyze the text, have created.

Placing Respondents by Category—Read the text of each of the respondents and place each response in the appropriate unit of analysis or category.

Count the Responses—After all respondent responses have been reviewed and categorized, count the number of respondents in each category.

Create a Composite Response—create a statement that reflects the content of all respondents in each category. These comments tend to be a generalization of all the responses within each category. The number of respondents in that category should be included in the statement.

Short Paragraph Response—In some cases, when the responses are complex or provide extensive data, a short paragraph may need to be created to provide a fair statement of the information provided.

EXAMPLE: ANALYZING PRE–POST DATA ACCORDING TO THE STANDARD OF SUCCESS

The way you write the "standard of success" in your objective will determine how you analyze your pre–post data. Consider the following examples for a tutoring program.

Example A: The letter grades of tutored students will increase by an average of ½ grade per semester.

Example B: 80% of tutored students will increase their letter grades by ½ or more per semester.

Each statement requires different information to be collected and different data analysis. Example A requires that the "average" (mean) letter grade increase by ½ grade or better when all students are grouped together. Example B requires that the percentage of students who increase their letter grades by ½ grade or more be greater than 80%. Example B therefore requires an additional piece of information, individual gains, while the first does not. In order to compute individual gain scores, you need to match each student's pre- and post-measures. (Note: It is always better to compute individual gain scores, when possible. However, an average increase can be computed in the absence of individual gain scores.)

Example A: "The letter grades of tutored students will increase by an average of ½ grade per semester."

The difference between the first semester average and the second semester average is .44 letter grades; therefore, the objective was not quite attained. Please note that the grades here are not paired by individual student. However, the group of students taking both the pre/post tests should be the same. If you are unsure that the group of students taking the pre/post tests is the same, you may want to get some help from a researcher to analyze your data.

First Semester		Second Semester	
D	= 1	C	= 2
D+	= 1.5	D-	= .7
C	= 2	B	= 3
B	= 3	B+	= 3.5
C+	= 2.5	B	= 3
Total	**= 10**	**Total**	**= 12.2**
n	**= 5**	**n**	**= 5**
Mean	**= 2**	**Mean**	**= 2.44**

Example B: "80% of tutored students will increase their letter grade by at least ½ grade per semester."

The preferred method of looking at pre-post data is to match each student's pre- and post-test scores. For this example, 4 out of 5 students gained ½ letter grades. The percentage of students gaining ½ letter grade (%=F/n) is 80%; therefore, the objective was attained.

	First Semester		Second Semester		Difference Pre–Post	.5 Letter Grade Gain?
Ann	D	= 1	C	= 2	+1	Yes
Bob	D+	= 1.5	D-	= .7	–.8	No
Chris	C	= 2	B	= 3	+1	Yes
Dot	B	= 3	B+	= 3.5	+.5	Yes
Ed	C+	= 2.5	B	= 3	+.5	Yes

Sources: Created by Project STAR.

Forming the questions to conduct a content analysis will determine how to categorize the responses. If the questions are asked in a manner that leads the respondents to answer clear direction, the unit of analysis has already been identified, based on the focus of the response. These are predetermined questions. If the questions were developed so that the respondent could respond in a number of different directions, and the answers themselves need to be reviewed and categorized to create the units of analysis, these are emergent questions. When developing the instruments for qualitative data, program staff should determine which type of questions to ask; this will determine how the unit of analysis will be identified. The examples in

To begin to organize data for content analysis, you must determine the categories you want to use. Read your organized responses. Decide whether you want to use any *predetermined* categories or if you want to use *emergent* categories. Identify your categories. It may help to write a brief description of what each category should contain. Remember to include an "other" category.

a) **Predetermined categories** are selected before the data comes back. They may be selected based on their importance to your program, or because they are included in the question generating the responses. For example, responses to "Explain why you did or did not enjoy this event," could be placed in "Enjoyed" or "Did Not Enjoy" categories.

b) **Emergent categories** are determined after several readings of the data. For example, if you ask students "What did you like about your tutor?", you may need to read the complete set of answers for this question several times before categories, such as "Consistency" or "Friendliness" appear.

Box 6.6 demonstrate the difference between how questions can be formed so that unit of analysis would be predetermined or emergent.

Summarizing the Data

After analyzing the data and finding the results of the evaluation conducted, the last phase is to develop statements of the findings. In most cases, the data can be answered in a number of different ways, allowing program staff to make a number of different statements. The manner in which the data is used and the type of statements made should correspond to the evaluation questions first developed when the evaluation was being planned. Program staff are encouraged to look at the data results in a number of different angles. Not only will program staff give themselves options on how they want to report their findings, they may also learn what worked best, as well as what didn't work so well, in their program services. This information can help program staff improve program service delivery, the main reason for using the empowerment evaluation approach to evaluate their program.

Reporting the Results

The reporting of evaluation results can be conducted using a number of different methods. The most common method is in a text document. However, reporting results can be conducted in other forms, such as oral reports, videos, or press releases. When planning for reporting evaluation results, consider the audience that the report is intended for. From there, program staff can determine both the method of reporting as well as what information should be emphasized.

T. Dietz and A. Westerfelt (1997) suggest the following process when planning for reporting results:

Decide which findings to present in the report and determine the order in which you will present them. Begin with general information and move to specific findings, reflecting the focus of your study. To help organize the presentation of findings, make two lists: primary findings and secondary findings. The primary findings should relate directly to the evaluation question and should be given the most attention in the narrative and visual presentations. (p. 152)

As Dietz and Westerfelt infer, the report should address the evaluation questions identified when the evaluation plan was in development at the beginning of the program year. Therefore, before writing the report, the evaluation plan should be reviewed and the information in the evaluation plan be included in the report.

Planning for the Report

Developing a report on the evaluation of program services includes more than reporting on the results found from the evaluation. The report should tell a story of why the evaluation was conducted, how it was implemented, what the findings were, and what will happen to program services as a result of the findings. A basic format for reporting results includes restating the objective, describing the progress toward achieving this objective, noting the evaluation activities that have been engaged, describing relevant evaluation data, and stating the ensuing changes based on the results found. A template that provides guidance on reporting evaluation results is demonstrated in Box 6.7.

A more detailed outline of reporting evaluation results is demonstrated in Box 6.8. Many research texts (Dietz & Westerfelt, 1997; Friedman, 1998; Royse, 1999; and Grinnell, Jr., 2001) have identified elements to be included when presenting the findings and developing a report.

Types of Reporting Methods

What has been described is only one method of reporting evaluation results—by a text report. However, program staff may be required to report using other methods such as conducting an oral presentation before a board or council, or submitting a press release to justify to the community what the program accomplished. Keep in mind that regardless of the method used to report evaluation results, you should design the report to the audience, and provide enough information to describe how the evaluation was conducted.

Summary

The last two steps of the five-step evaluation process are data analysis and reporting of results. These two steps generally occur at the end of the program year; however, they should be planned and scheduled at the beginning of the program year. As dictated by the empowerment evaluation approach, program staff will be analyzing the data. Therefore, the analysis should remain simple, focusing on single-variable analysis. Both quantitative and qualitative analyses are described in this chapter. Reporting evaluation results can be conducted in many forms. Knowing who your audience is, focusing on the primary findings, and formatting your report effectively are key points in planning for your report.

References

Atherton, C., & Klemmack, D. (1982). *Research methods in social work: An introduction.* Lexington, MA: D.C. Heath and Company.

Dietz, T., & Westerfelt, A. (1997). *Planning and conducting agency-based research: A workbook for social work students in field placements.* New York: Longman.

Friedman, B. (1998). *The research tool kits: Putting it all together.* Pacific Grove, CA: Brooks/Cole.

Grinnell, Jr., R. (2001). *Social work research and evaluation: Quantitative approaches* (6th ed.). Itasca, IL: F.E. Peacock.

Royse, D. (1999). *Research methods in social work* (3rd ed.). Belmont, CA: Wadsworth.

BOX
6.7   **REPORTING FORM**

Using the outline provided, please complete the following information about progress towards your objectives during this reporting period.

I. Restate your objective:

_____

_____

II. Describe your progress toward achieving this objective during this reporting period.

A. Describe your activity, beneficiaries, and the number of people served this quarter and year to date.

_____

_____

B. Describe your desired result and indicators used to measure the desired result.

_____

_____

III. Note evaluation activities in which you have engaged.

A. Describe how you measured your desired result.

_____

_____

B. Describe who administered and completed the instruments.

_____

_____

IV. Describe relevant evaluation data.

A. Describe the results of your analysis of your evaluation data. (This should be related to the standard you set in your objectives.)

1. Results (include statistics and qualitative information).

_____

_____

2. Stories which illustrate your statistics or qualitative information.

_____

_____

B. Compare the results of your evaluation with the standard set in your objective.

_____

_____

V. State ideas for improvement in your program, or any next steps.

_____

_____

_____

Sources: Created by Project STAR. Used with permission of Aguirre International.

BOX
6.8
PRESENTATION OF FINDINGS AND REPORTING

A. Introduction and evaluation questions.

  Explain the rationales for the evaluation, the major questions that it intends to study, and what has been conducted. Basically, the report will include what was done and why, and the findings and what they mean.

B. Methodology and data collection strategies.
  1. Research design and data collection procedure:
      - Restate the purpose of the study and its major evaluation questions.
      - Describe the overall evaluation approach and how data were collected.
      - Describe how each question or program objective is being evaluated and how data are collected.
      - Identify variables to be measured.
      - Explain how ethical considerations are safeguarded.
  2. Sampling and target population:
      - Illustrate who is involved in the study, their characteristics, and how they are recruited or excluded.
      - Describe any sampling procedure involved, if any.
  3. Data collection instruments and analyses:
      - Identify variables to be measured and indicators that are used to measure changes.
      - Explain data collection instruments and their associated data analysis approaches.

C. Findings and results.
  1. Provide an executive summary of evaluation findings.
  2. Succinctly present main and secondary evaluation findings based on the analyses of data collected.
  3. Present findings according to evaluation questions or service objectives.
  4. Employ various data presentation methods (i.e., narrative, graphics, etc.) to display data for various audiences.

D. Discussions and implications for practice.
  1. Interpret the findings in relation to the evaluation questions; review how well the evaluation questions are being addressed.
  2. Identify limitations of the study and other possible theoretical, practical, and research design-related limitations.
  3. Describe how the findings could be incorporated for program improvement, new program plan, and other practical issues, including termination or changes of the programs.
  4. Discuss the utilities and implication of the evaluation and its findings for human service professionals, social workers, clients, and policy makers.
  5. Reflect on what has been learned from this process.
  6. Provide recommendations and suggestions for future studies.

E. Bibliography and appendices.

PUTTING IT TOGETHER: MODEL PROGRAM AND EVALUATION PLANS

In the previous chapters, different examples were used to illustrate our discussions on program planning, grant writing, and program evaluation. This chapter draws on the examples of three model plans to: (a) show the incorporation of information that we presented into program and evaluation plans, and (b) highlight the importance and seriousness of ethical considerations in carrying out program evaluation.

These models are intended to serve as examples or sample products of what they could be like. They are not standards or models of perfection for everyone to follow. Instead, they can serve as practical examples and references for readers to use in developing their very own program and evaluation plan.

Model #1, Project Healthy Families, represents a detailed program plan and evaluation plan for a federally funded demonstration program. It is a substance abuse prevention project targeting homeless children and their families. Evaluation tasks are to be carried out by a team of external evaluators.

Model #2, ABC AmeriCorps Project, represents a simple program evaluation plan for a small, local AmeriCorps service project. The project uses AmeriCorps members and volunteers to provide tutoring and other academic support activities to improve the reading abilities of at-risk students. Evaluation tasks are to be carried out by program staff.

Model #3, Ethical Considerations (for Project Hope), shows how ethical considerations in program evaluation are detailed and observed. Ethical practice is an essential component of any evaluation plan. Project Hope is a substance abuse treatment program focused on Asian-American youth. Its confidentiality and ethical concerns represent a relatively detailed write-up that may not be required for smaller evaluation tasks; however, the basic ethical practices and safeguards are still expected to be followed and valued in smaller programs.

Model #1: Project Healthy Families

Program Plan and Description

The Good Place, Inc., proposes a 3-year demonstration project—"Healthy Families"—targeting 800 rural homeless and low-income families and their children and adolescents (ages 0–14) in Springdale. This project will test the efficiency and effectiveness of a set of theoretically based, innovative, and well-coordinated programs that are specific to gender, age, and culture of the target population. These programs aim to promote the current goals set by the Center for Substance Abuse Prevention (CSAP).

The working hypothesis for this project is that "empowering the target population to increase family stability and to promote children and family wellness will decrease the likelihood of involvement in alcohol, tobacco, and other drugs (ATOD) use and other related high-risk behaviors." In other words, children and parents who have stable living arrangements, positive bonding with significant others, congruent self-identities, and the skills to maintain family and individual economic and social well-being are less likely to be involved in ATOD use and other high-risk or violent behaviors. This project targets homeless/low-income families and their children living at the Good Place's housing (emergency shelter and transitional apartments) and in the surrounding low-income neighborhoods.

The theoretical base for the proposed project rely mostly on the Family Health Model (Pardeck & Yuen, 1999), which also includes three major perspectives: ecological (Germain & Gitterman, 1987; Meyer, 1983), family systems (Hartman & Laird, 1983; Von Bertalanffy, 1968), and social constructionist (Gelber & Specter, 1987; Gergen & McNamee, 1992; Hoffman, 1990). This combined ecological systems and social constructionist approach views homeless/low-income children's high-risk behaviors from a holistic and dynamic perspective.

Pardeck and Yuen (1999) define family health as "a state of holistic well-being of the family system. Family health is manifested by the development of, and continuous interaction among, the physical, mental, emotional, social, economic, cultural, and spiritual dimensions of the family which results in its holistic well-being as well as that of its members" (p. 1). Family health intervention skills include: developmental assessment, resource linkage, supportive intervention, supportive intervention, confrontational intervention, empowerment of the client, use of social learning approaches, recognizing the level of prevention and readiness for change, utilization of the family unit as change agent, understanding and assessing the construction of a client's reality, and advocating for the client.

Ecological perspective assesses individuals through the context of one's interaction with the environment. Homeless and low-income children and families occupy a "negative niche" in today's society. Some view them as "lazy people" who drain and waste American resources. Meanwhile, their homeless and poverty situations have posed a variety of life stressors that are often traumatic and detrimental. Unfortunately, many of them may not have the required educational and life skills that allow them to cope properly with these stress factors. As a result, many choose alternative coping approaches, which may not be effective or acceptable by society.

Systems theory uses circular causality and views that an individual and her or his environment interact and affect each other mutually. Through input, throughput, output, and feedback, units within the system seek for equilibrium. Often, this feedback system for homeless and low-income children and families has been either absent, negative, or nonfunctional. Both ecological perspectives and systems theory stress the importance of the reciprocal relationship between individual and family as well as the "wellness" of the systems and their interaction processes.

The social constructionist approach believes that stories, myths, literature, and legends help individuals draw the events of their lives into meaningful wholes that have structure, direction, and purpose. These creations help them to know who they are, how they cope with failure and success, and most importantly, where they are heading—the new reality. Homeless children and parents are likely to become more self-sufficient if they can have pride in themselves and see that there is hope for their future.

Many homeless children and adolescents are living in the stage of anomie. These anomic youngsters are likely to turn to other subcultures to meet their needs for affiliation and may become involved in high-risk behaviors such as substance abuse and gang activities. Individuals who can identify with a stable living arrangement will likely encounter fewer adjustment and personal problems.

The proposed interventions are also based on the risk/protective factors applied to four domains: individual, families, peers, and schools. The proposed strategies are intended to improve stability and life skills of homeless or low-income children and their families. The proposed Healthy Families Project has three main components: (a) Family Together, (b) Health and Case Management, and (c) Community and School Services.

The **Family Together** component consists of four main sets of interrelated activities.

1. During the regular school year, from around 3:15 to 4:30 P.M., targeted children will participate in the After-School Learning Center, which is located within the shelter and will provide a variety of tutorial and recreational activities.
2. While these children are attending the center's activities, their parents (mostly mothers) will attend a separate Parents-to-Parents program, which provides educational and employment readiness activities.
3. Twice a week, after the dinner and individual family hours from 4:30 to 6:00 P.M., children and their families will come together to participate in the Family Night program. This program is based on the Family Success curriculum for homeless families and aims to strengthen family functioning and resiliency factors.
4. Once a month, special events such as trips to the Six Flags amusement park and local festivals will be organized to provide opportunities for family fun and interaction.

The **Health and Case Management** component assists targeted families' abilities to coordinate their health/mental health, employment, and social needs. This component includes three main services:

1. Basic health check-up, medical care, and referral services provided on-site at the shelter or through referral to the local St. Francis Hospital.
2. Individual and group counseling and advocacy.
3. Employment and goal-setting assistance.

The **Community and School** component facilitates comprehensive support from schools and communities to promote healthy families. This component consists of four main activities:

1. Implementation of an Alateen or peer support group for targeted children at Johnson Middle School.
2. Coordination with school officials to develop a mechanism to monitor the academic and overall performance of targeted children from the shelter.
3. Development of a volunteer service group for the project by local college students and youth.
4. Development of an eight-member Health Families Advisory Board. The board consists of parents from the target population, human service providers, a representative of religious groups, a law enforcement officer, a school representative, and community leaders.

Program Evaluation

The objectives of the evaluation plan are: (a) to document and monitor the implementation of the proposed interventions and activities, and (b) to provide data to assess the outcome and overall impact of the proposed project. The results of evaluation will provide information for better understanding of the three key questions for the proposed project:

1. Can a comprehensive and culturally competent project that addresses the multiple needs of participants lead to the reduction of the use of alcohol, tobacco, and other drugs

(ATOD) as well as related problems among target homeless/low-income families? If so, what strategies or combinations of strategies produce the best results?

2. What are the relationships between ATOD-related problems and family capacity?
3. Can this proposed model be replicated elsewhere?

These three questions relate directly to Center for Substance Abuse Prevention's (CSAP) requirements, and to the proposed application's goals and objectives. They will also serve as principles for process and outcome evaluation.

The evaluation team will meet with the project management staff during the first month of the project to further refine the following evaluation action plan. Project staff will then review this revised action plan, and a youth focus group and a parent focus group will provide comments. Their input will help refine the definition of risk and resiliency factors and further determine the focus of evaluation. The revised action plan will be finalized in the third month.

Process Evaluation

Documenting and monitoring the planning, implementation, and interrelationship of the components of the proposed project are the focus of the process evaluation, which aims to: (a) describe program interventions' development, implementation, and activities, (b) provide quantitative and qualitative data on services delivered and their effectiveness, and (c) document the appropriateness and acceptability of the program within the target community. To achieve these aims, there are three main components of the process evaluation: (a) program planning and development, (b) program interventions, and (c) database management system.

A. Program Planning and Development   Planning and development is an ongoing process. The documentation of this process includes compiling information on administrative planning, staff meeting, staff recruitment and training, preparation for program activity, work schedule, organizational support, and community linkage. This information not only documents the progress of the project, but also provides a basis for a more accurate definition of the problems to be addressed and their associated risk and protective factors.

In order to document the process of program development and implementation, the evaluation team will collect agendas of project staff meetings, minutes, and other related documents. Evaluation team staff will also participate in selected planning and program activities in order to do observations. Staff and participants will be interviewed, in addition to the biannual questionnaire responses, to document satisfaction measures and other concerns. Staff training, workshops, and conferences will also be documented through records of participation and minutes of discussions. Encounter forms and attendance sheets will document participation and units of service. CSAP Management Information Forms (MIF) require specific information about the target population. The evaluation team will collect relevant data for MIF.

B. Program Interventions   The documentation of program intervention should provide both qualitative and quantitative descriptions of the interventions. These documentation procedures include several elements and different data collection approaches. First, descriptions of type of interventions will be recorded along with intervention products such as curriculum. Second, intake and application forms will be used to collect information about project participants. Third, quantity and utilization of project services, as well as the time and locations of these services, will be documented through encounter forms, activity logs, and attendance sheets. Fourth, both staff and project participants will complete satisfaction survey scales to provide feedback and assessment regarding the project. Fifth, some ethnographic observations of project activities will be used to collect qualitative information for the project. These process evaluation procedures provide a basis for the understanding of the operation and effectiveness of the project. The following are some of the measures and forms used to document these operations and their effectiveness:

Staff Recruitment, Hiring, and Training   Recruitment and hiring procedures, as well as staff training and conferences, will be documented. Feedback from staff through interviews and questionnaires will also be collected.

Planning and Development   Activity forms, meeting agendas and minutes, and participatory observation will be used to reflect program development process, problems encountered, and alternatives and solutions to the problems.

Program Usage   Attendance records, activity logs, sign-in and sign-out forms, and daily self-reports by staff will be used to document the extent of service used, the achievements and barriers, client flow, client penetration, and the characteristics of project participants.

Participant and Staff Satisfaction   Project staff and project participants, particularly those in instructional activities, will be asked to provide feedback through questionnaires and interviews. Information collected provides a basis to assess the level of satisfaction toward project activities and organizational and community support.

Target Population   The agency's current General Data Form collects basic demographic information, including ethnicity, gender, age, family composition, employment and income, and other data. It will be revised to become the intake and application forms for the project. The new forms will include information on risk categories, ATOD histories, and special health concerns. This form will be continuously updated and revised upon review of clients' needs and staff's recommendation.

Program Outreach   All individual and community outreach will be tracked by an outreach encounter form. Content, frequency, and results of these efforts will be documented to assess effectiveness.

Case Management Recording   Case management services for participants will be recorded in individual clients' charts. General social work case management recording requirements will be applied as the standard for charting. These recordings will document the type and progress of interventions, intervention achievements and barriers, frequency and characteristics of referrals, interorganizational linkages, and assessment of clients and services provided.

Linkages with Managed Health Care   Project linkages with local managed health care providers at all levels will be documented. The City of Springdale has three major regional health centers and an array of other specialized medical care facilities. It is the mecca of medical service in the region. Project's linkages with these managed health care systems will be documented from individual client referrals to institutional agreements. Special attention will be placed on how these linkages will affect the provision of prevention services provided by these organizations.

Project Goals and Objectives   Each objective's and activity's progress will be collected on a quarterly basis. In addition to the use of forms and self-reports from clients and staff, participatory observation by evaluation team staff will also be used for data collection.

For Objective 1 (Families Together Component), for its After-School Learning Center activities, process evaluation will document all planning meetings, site development and selection meetings, activities, minutes, and attendance records. For the Parents-to-Parents program, a pre- and posttest will be used to document changes in participants' attitude and knowledge about parenting and other life skills. Attendance and dropout records will also be used. Family Night and Family Fun activities will be documented by types of activities, attendance, and an observation of interaction among family members. In addition to attendance records and self-reported evaluation from staff and participants, a client satisfaction form will also be used. This survey form will be developed and used by the ninth month of the project.

For Objective 2, Health and Case Management, units of counseling or health screening and medical intervention, as well as referral will be recorded. A case management chart and a medical service chart that record intervention process and other related activities will be opened for each client. Types of health and mental health concerns for project participants will be categorized for baseline data and trend analysis. The project's involvement in the development of the local managed care system will be documented through minutes and agendas. Prevention services developed by local health care providers as the result of interaction with the proposed project will be tracked and documented.

For Objective 3, School/Community Services, project staff will visit participants' teachers (with the approval of participants' parents) to obtain students' academic records to develop baseline and progress data for comparison. Volunteer group activities will be documented for training model development meetings, training contents and implementation, attendance records, service provided, time used, and volunteer application forms and screening procedures. Teen Support Groups' activity types and contents, attendance, recruitment and retention records, and the extent of involvement from volunteers will be recorded. Data on the Advisory Board's membership composition, meeting minutes and agendas, and types of involvement will be collected.

Cost Analysis: The evaluation team will analyze the cost per unit of service and client. Cost analysis is to evaluate the efficiency of the project and the relationship between efforts and effects. Its results will be compared among various project components and to other similar prevention projects. Data collected for each component will include: number of clients served, units of service provided, staff time used, personnel and operating cost, and volunteer and other in-kind support.

C. Database Management Information System   A well-developed database management information system (MIS) provides the mechanism to store and compile quantifiable data to assess the development and effectiveness of the project. This system involves: (a) the development of file formats and identification of appropriate software, (b) subsequent data entry, and (c) the generation of reports. With data collection and data analyses, the MIS forms the basis for evaluation.

All clients are required to complete an intake or application form to collect basic demographic and ATOD use-related information. Encounter and attendance forms will collect units and types of services for individual, group, case management, and family activities detailing date of occurrence, numbers served, location, and time. Client chart documentation, including the *DSM-IV* diagnosis (if applicable), will also serve as process data. Satisfaction scales will provide input and feedback from clients, families, and staff. Observation field notes, pre/post tests results, and other measures will also be stored in the MIS. All project forms and measures will be updated as needed; baseline and other project data will continue to be collected throughout the project years. Other data, which are available from local private and government organizations, will also be utilized for comparison.

Although the evaluation team has the primary responsibility for the development and maintenance of the MIS, it is a joint effort between evaluation and project staff to manage this system. Basic database software, including Microsoft Access and the Statistical Package for Social Science (SPSS), will be used.

Outcome Evaluation

Based on the project's ecological systems social constructionist theoretical orientations and its focus on the individual, family, peer, and school domains, the outcome evaluation will provide better understanding to the three key evaluation questions: effectiveness of intervention strategies, ATOD use and family capacity, and replicability of project.

A sectional time series design with nonrandomized comparison groups, with age and gender cohorts over a period of 3 years, will be used to assess changes. Outcome objectives listed previously, including family functioning and stability, academic readiness, family and school bonding, self-image, peer relations and support, physical and mental wellness, and ATOD use and other deviance behaviors, will be assessed. Variables such as frequency and types of intervention, duration and nature of participation in various interventions, and individual and family psychosocial histories are also assessed for their impact on the outcome of the project.

All project participants will be involved in this evaluation through three evaluation cycles (see Box 7.1). A pretest will be administered to all new participants (age 8 and above) during the first month of their enrollment; the posttest will be administrated 6 months later, or when the clients leave the program if their participation is more than 1 month; and the posttest 2 will be administrated on the twelfth month. A guided interview will be scheduled on the sixth month after the posttest. Minimally, changes over a period of a year will be assessed. Pre- and posttest measures will be implemented in two or more sessions over the period of 2 weeks to avoid weardown. Project staff and volunteers will assist both children and adults individually to complete forms, pretest, and posttest to address literacy issues and to ensure correct understanding of the questions. For children younger than age 8, observations of their drawings and play will be used to assess changes. Assistance and training from art and play therapists will be used to develop project staff's capability (see Box 7.1 for a schedule of evaluations).

Due to the transient nature of the target population, it will be difficult to have a stable intervention group or a matching group for study. Two approaches will be used to deal with this issue. First, 30 children who participate in project activities will be compared annually to an external comparison group of 30 students. This comparison group will be composed of students in the Johnson school who are not clients of this agency's services but are comparable in general characteristics of children of the intervention group. Variables to be assessed will include academic readiness, peer relations and support, family and school bonding, physical and mental wellness, and ATOD use and other deviance behaviors. Approval for participation will need to be obtained from parents of students of both groups in order to conduct pre- and posttests. Second, intervention group participants who are involved in the project on a regular basis for at least 6 months will be compared to a comparison group consisting of participants who are involved in only a part of the project during a particular time (e.g., summer program) or only involved in regular programs for a period of 1–3 months.

TABLE 7.1	SCHEDULE OF EVALUATIONS					
Project Month	**1st**	**6th**	**12th**	**18th**	**24th**	**30th**
Cycle 1	Pretest	Posttest 1	Posttest 2	Interview	Interview	Interview
Cycle 2		Pretest	Posttest 1	Posttest 2	Interview	Interview
Cycle 3			Pretest	Posttest 1	Posttest 2	Interview

For participants in the comparison groups who are 12 years of age and older, outcome assessment will also measure whether there are decreases in the incidence, frequency, and amount of ATOD uses and their related violence. Additionally, participants' perception of the effects (harm) of ATOD uses and relationships to the total well being of the individuals will be evaluated.

Finally, a random subset of 30 youngsters (15, ages 6–11; 15, ages 12–14), 15 each for the first two years, will be tracked for 24 months to provide information on the long-range effects of the project.

Project participants will be given $5 to $10 or certificates to local food establishments as incentives to participate in each of the pre- and posttests and interviews.

Measures   The reliability and validity of applying standard instruments to low-income, transient, or homeless populations have been a concern for this project. Modification of these instruments for specific culture/class, age group, literacy level, and language poses the same concerns for validity; it is, however, a necessary step toward more culturally appropriate evaluation. The evaluation team plans to validate and revise all proposed measures during the first 6 months to ensure cultural appropriateness, content validity, and reliability.

Outcome forms being considered include:

- *Index of Self-Esteem* (Hudson, 1982), a 25-item measure on self-image, self-confidence, and self-satisfaction.
- *Symptom Check List* (SCL-90-R), a 90-item measure by Derogatis (1992) for psychological well-being.
- *AIDS Risks Reduction* (ARR), developed by Springdale County Health Department based on fact sheets provided by the Center for Disease Control and Prevention will be used for HIV and AIDS risk assessment.
- *Self-Report Family Inventory* (SFI), developed by the local Family Service Council, will be used to measure family competence, style, and relationships.
- *Academic Self-Concept from the Effective School Battery* (Gottfredson, 1982) will be used to assess attachment to school and education expectation.
- *Substance Use Inventory* (SUI) is a widely used self-report measure of the patterns of substance use among youth (Skager, Fisher, & Maddahian, 1986).
- *High Risk Behaviors Inventory* (Jessor & Jessor, 1977) assesses frequency of high-risk behaviors.
- *Social/Interpersonal Skills Questionnaire* (to be developed by the evaluation team) is a 26-item measure that assesses social/interpersonal skills, shame, face, and community relationship.

- *Social Support Questionnaire Short Form* (SSQ), developed by the Academic University Social Research Center, will help identify social support patterns.
- *Family Stability/Homelessness Questionnaire* (to be developed by the evaluation team) measures the length, type, and frequency of homelessness and its various impacts.
- *Satisfaction Questionnaire* (to be developed by the evaluation team) measures the degree of satisfaction of service and the effectiveness of services.

Implementation schedule, target respondents, time requirements, and purposes of these measures are described in Box 7.2.

Additionally, established assessment tools for programs and curriculum (e.g., the Nurturing Parenting Programs) used in the Healthy Families project will be used during program implementation to measure effectiveness and appropriateness of these programs.

Data Analysis and Reports   On a quarterly basis, information including descriptions and data collected will be reviewed and analyzed. Data will be entered into a state-of-the-art desktop computer and analyzed with updated database and spreadsheet software (Access and SPSS). Descriptive statistics and inferential statistics, as well as analyses of variances, will be utilized to measure program effectiveness and impact. These analyses will determine if there are significant differences between comparison groups and between pre- and posttests. To assess overall program impact and its influence on prevention programs of other health care providers, meta-analysis and trend analysis will be conducted to evaluate the extent of the impact. During the first year, quarterly reports to the project management will be submitted. Starting in the second year, reports will be prepared on a biannual and annual basis. Biannual and annual reports will discuss problems encountered, options attempted, and solutions presented.

Evaluation Team

The evaluation team will be headed by Dr. Frank Kellen, a professor of social work at the Academic University in Springdale, CA. He received the university's 2001 Outstanding Instructor Award for his excellent teaching in his graduate-level social research courses. He has many years of experience in working with high-risk populations, and more than 10 years of experience in working with CSAP and its projects. Kellen was a principal investigator for a CSAP high-risk youth project and a Center for Substance Abuse Treatment (CSAT) outpatient treatment project. He also helped in the development and implementation of a CSAP violence prevention project. Kellen has been involved in various National Institute of Drug Abuse (NIDA) and CSAP research projects. Currently, he is a project evaluator for the Service U.S.A. program. Dr. Kellen will report to Ms. Lovejoy, chief executive officer of the agency.

The evaluation team will be a subcontractor of the project. It will include one part-time research associate who will be either a Ph.D. or doctoral student in human service area, and a part-time research assistant. The evaluation team will have regular biweekly meetings. It will also meet with project staff management once every 2 weeks prior to their meeting with the whole project staff. The evaluation team staff will attend initial project planning and implementation meetings as well as selected program activities for observational measures.

Confidentiality

All information will be kept in the evaluation computer and in a locked file cabinet with access only by evaluation staff and the project director. All evaluation materials will be kept strictly confidential as required by the Federal Register, General Provisions Title 42, Chapter 1, Part 2. All

TABLE 7.2	IMPLEMENTATION SCHEDULE OF OUTCOME MEASURES

Time of Assessment	Variable (# of items)	Data Source	Length of Admin.	Measure
Pre and Post	Self-image, satisfaction (25)	Children and Youth (C and Y) ages 8–14	10 min.	Index of Self-Esteem
Pre and Post	Health status (90)	C and Y 8–14 and Parents	20 min.	Symptom Check List
Pre and Post	HIV and AIDS (15)	C and Y 8–14 and Parents	10 min.	AIDS Risks Reduction
Pre and Post	Family style and competency (34)	C and Y 8–14	15 min.	Self-Report Family Inventory
Pre and Post	School attachment and expectation (12)	C and Y 8–14	5 min.	Academic Self-Concept
Pre and Post	ATOD use behavioral patterns (22)	C and Y 8–14 and Parents	10 min.	Substance Use Inventory
Pre and Post	Frequency of high-risk behaviors (14)	C and Y 8–14	5 min.	High Risk Behaviors Inventory
Pre and Post, Interview	Social skills, shame, support (26)	C and Y 8–14 Parents	10 min.	Social/Interpersonal Skills Questionnaire
Pre and Post, Interview	Social support (12)	Parents	5 min.	Social Support Questionnaire Short Form
Pre, Interview	Stability, effects of homelessness (35)	Parents	15 min.	Family Stability/ Homelessness Questionnaire
Post, Interview	Satisfaction and effectiveness (35)	Clients and Staff	15 min.	Satisfaction Questionnaire

forms will utilize numerical codes for identification kept separately. Participation will be strictly voluntary and subject to a signed consent form that will identify all factors related to evaluation including the testing procedures. Consent is required from all parents and youth as well as family members involved in pre- and posttest assessments. Risks are not anticipated, but we will inform clients about the nature of instruments and the approximate length of time for test completion. Please see the ethical considerations section of this proposal for further discussion of confidentiality and participant protection.

Model #2: Evaluation Plan for ABC Agency AmeriCorps Project

Objectives of the Evaluation Tasks

1. Provide ongoing process data for reporting and improvement. (Are we doing what we set out to do?)

2. Assess the outcomes/effectiveness of program activities. (How well do we do?)
3. Assess the impacts of the program. (So what?)

Information Management System

The project will develop a data collection system to store and compile quantifiable process and outcome data to evaluate the project. The project will also use specific forms for different objectives, a key informant survey, interview guides, a focus group guide, the meeting agenda and minutes, and other written reports to document qualitative and quantitative information.

The project will recruit a volunteer or part-time data processing person to collect, aggregate, and analyze program evaluation data. The project will approach local organizations or universities to identify this assistant person.

Process Evaluation

Program Planning and Development   This evaluation process includes compiling information on administrative planning, activity development meetings, member recruitment and training, activity preparations, schedules, organization support, community linkages, problems encountered, and alternatives and solutions to problems. The project staff and members will collect activity logs, agendas, minutes, reports, and other documents as the basis for reports.

Program Interventions
1. *Members and Partners Recruitment and Training.*   The project director will document the recruitment and training of volunteer members and partner organizations. Feedback from members and partners on orientation and training will be collected through a post-event Training Evaluation Form.
2. *Program Usage.*   The Volunteer Application Form and Volunteer and Service Recipient Sign-In forms will be used to document the extent of service used, achievements made, barriers faced, participant flow and penetration, and the characteristics of project participants.
3. *Target Population.*   The project will collect and analyze target population data, including gender, age, race, and academic performance. Data will be collected through volunteer records, sign-in and sign-out forms, and information provided by partner organizations.
4. *Community Linkage.*   The Community Encounter Form, community meetings, and activity records will track individual and community outreach. These records will include the date, person contacted, organization, content, frequency, and results of these efforts to assess the extent and effectiveness. Other community collaboration efforts will be tracked by meeting minutes, service contracts, memorandum of understanding, and the frequency and type of participation by various community members or agencies.
5. *Project Objectives.*   Each objective and its evaluation strategies are detailed in the attached Objective and Evaluation Plan Form (as seen previously in Box 3.11).

Outcome Evaluation

The project will utilize the evaluation or assessment strategies described previously in the Project Objectives to provide process and outcome measures for each of the program objectives within the three main program categories. These categories are: (a) Getting Things Done, (b) Member Development, and (c) Community Strengthening.

"Getting Things Done" Category

1. *America Reads Component Objective*

   a. Use the America Reads Participation Form (ARPF) to document the usage of tutoring services by students. These will include the number of hours of service provided, area of study, as well as frequency and comment of participation. If readily available and with proper consents, volunteers and program administration should consider collecting participating students' scores on a standardized test used by the school at the beginning of the school year/semester and then at the end. Volunteers will also assess students' performance on reading and other skills through observations.

   b. Use the Tutorial Goal Information Form (TGIF) to document the extent of achievement of tutorial goals by each student. This information will compliment the narrative comments to provide a better assessment of students' academic performance. Students are encouraged to be involved in identifying items included in the form that will assess them.

2. *Volunteer Development Component Objective*

   a. Use the Positive Self-Development Form (PSDF) to assess the development of volunteers over the three major areas of development every 4 months. These areas include Knowledge, Skills (Individual, Team/Leadership, Community/Planning), and Personal/Attitude. Volunteers will be involved in the development of the form.

   b. Develop a Parent Satisfaction Survey form and a Teacher Satisfaction Survey form to document the level of satisfaction and suggestions for improvement for the project at the end of each academic year. Program directors will use a Training Evaluation Form as a sample to develop these Satisfaction Survey Forms. They should also use the forms (e.g., activity log) to document the extent of participation by parents and teachers.

"Members Development" Category

   a. Use the Member Development Portfolio Form during initial meeting/orientation, and again at 6 months and at 12 months to develop baseline data and to assess AmeriCorps members' developments in each of the areas identified.

   b. Use a Leadership Assessment and Civic Involvement Scale at the beginning and the end of the program year to evaluate members' growth in these two areas.

"Community Strengthening" Category

Evaluation data will be collected through the use of the aforementioned forms and other existing forms. Program staff will:

   a. Use a Community Encounter Form, Training Evaluation Form, Volunteer Application Form, and other meeting minutes and materials to document the extent, type, frequency, nature, and results of project's community contacts.

   b. Use of focus group meetings and key informant interviews to collect qualitative data.

Impact Evaluation

Based on the project objectives and their process and outcome evaluation results, program staff will identify and assess the areas and the extent of program impacts. This assessment will be further supported by information collected through end-of-the-year focus-group meetings with specific target populations including community representatives, service recipients, and Agency ABC members. The program will use key informant interviews and a "Top 10 list"-styled approach to promote discussions.

Sampling Plan and Analysis Plan

The evaluation plan for this project may require simple sampling procedures. Sampling, however, can be done on a three-tier level, if the program wishes to draw a sample to evaluate any portion of the program. This will include: (a) all participants for a particular activity, (b) participants who attend activities consistently, and (c) a percentage of the consistent participants who are selected by a random approach.

Basically, the analysis plan the program needs to develop an information management system/database to store evaluation data. The program should update all process data on a regular basis. Single-variable analysis, measurements of central tendency and dispersion (e.g., frequency distribution, percentage, mean, mode, median, minimum, maximum, and range) could be used to interpret data collected. Outcome data will be collected through the aforementioned forms. Analysis of changes can be achieved through basic observation and calculation of increase or decrease, single variable analyses, and central tendency measurements and comparisons.

Implementation of Evaluation
1. The program will contact local organizations and universities to recruit a student who will assist in the data input and analysis.
2. The program should develop a functional database to store and compile quantifiable process and outcome data to evaluate the project.
3. The program will provide specific orientation sessions to AmeriCorps members on the purpose and the implementation of evaluation. It will also schedule specific times during each week for members to complete evaluation tasks.
4. Develop the sense of ownership and buy-in by the partner agencies, members, and volunteers.

Model #3: Confidentiality and Ethical Considerations

New Horizon Association has long-established stringent guidelines regarding confidentiality of all records and charts of clients. Policies and procedures are written, reviewed on an annual basis, and subject to change following current health and mental health licensing procedures of Noble County, the State of Massachusetts, Center for Substance Abuse Prevention, and all federal guidelines.

Target Population
1. Project Hope will target Vietnamese, Cambodian, Filipino, and Amerasian adolescents, ages 13–21, in South Worthington who have misused and/or abused alcohol, tobacco, and other drugs. Asian Americans account for 7% (7,000) of the county's population (roughly 100,000), and 60% (4,200) of them live in the city of Worthington. Asian Americans make up 15% of the city's population (28,000). Vietnamese (2,000) and Filipinos (1,500) are the two largest Asian groups in the city, while Cambodian (500) and Amerasian (200) are the often-neglected groups due to their smaller populations. About 12% of the targeted ethnic

groups are adolescents between the ages of 13-21; among them 54% are male and 46% are female. More than half of the target populations are immigrants or refugees. Detailed descriptions of the target population based on socioeconomic status, culture, and other factors are reviewed in the *Target Population* Section in the proposal.

2. Criteria for inclusion of participants into the substance abuse treatment component of Project Hope include: (a) being Asian-American residents of Noble County age 13–21, (b) having presenting problems of substance abuse, (c) determination of relevance based on the required assessment tools, (d) willingness to commit to entering and participating in the treatment program, (e) willingness to obtain a general medical physical, and (f) demonstration that there is no proclivity to violence. Services at the program's Wellness Center are open to all clients interested in receiving medical services. Clients with a dual diagnosis of mental illness and substance abuse will be served in conjunction with the agency's Mental Health Treatment Program.

Applicants may be found ineligible when they are physically/medically unsuitable for the services, are prone to violent behaviors, or have a history of arson.

Participant Recruitment and Selection

1. Criteria for inclusion or exclusion. See the Target Population section in this proposal.
2. Clients for Project Hope will be recruited through various New Horizon Association programs, local health care providers, government agencies and related programs, education and ethnic community groups, and self-referrals. Project staff will conduct outreach to target ethnic groups to provide community education and recruitment. New Horizon Association's current clients outreach and recruitment policies will be used and revised for the proposed project.
3. Participation in this project is strictly voluntary. Clients can withdraw from the program at any time. Court-ordered individuals are also free to leave the program. However, the program may be required to inform proper criminal justice authorities regarding these client' departures. Individuals who are involuntarily discharged from the program may appeal to the principal investigator or executive director for a review of the decision.

Data Collection

- Data will be collected from participants, their parents, and staff by means of intake records, drug abuse assessment instruments, written questionnaires, and service logs.
- Detailed description on individuals from whom data will be collected is discussed in this proposal's *Evaluation* section.
- Copies of standard data collection instruments that will be used for this project are provided in the Appendix.

Privacy and Confidentiality

The current New Horizon Association Personnel Policies, Outpatient Mental Health Program Policies, and Substance Abuse Treatment Program Policies all contain procedures that ensure compliance with local, state, and federal laws and regulations on clients' privacy and confidentiality. These confidentiality policies also regulate access of all charts, files, and information regarding clients. They will be extended to Project Hope.

The policies and all corresponding procedures are in accordance with the Federal Register, General Provisions of Title 42, Chapter 1, Part 2. All clients are required to sign a consent form indicating their willingness to participate in the treatment program prior to their enrollment. Clients will also be requested to sign a second consent form to indicate their participation in the collection of evaluative data for the program. However, no clients will be refused for services if they are unwilling to take part in the evaluation. Court ordered clients will be required to sign an additional consent form for the program to inform proper criminal justice authorities on their status.

Participation in the program and its evaluation is voluntary. Clients will be informed of their rights, both verbally and in writing, as well as the voluntary nature of their participation. They will also be informed about their rights to revoke their consent and that no privileges will be denied if they refuse to consent.

The consent forms state who is releasing the information, who will be receiving the information, and what specific information will be disclosed for what purpose. The consents are time limited, and clients can revoke their consent at any time. Both the client and the program staff need to sign and date the consent forms.

All client charts and records will be kept in separate locked files and are stored in a locked room accessible only to staff with clear sign-out privileges. No charts should be kept on staff desks or shelves, unless being actively used.

Through a coding system, client data will be stored and used for evaluation and to ensure privacy and confidentiality. Identifiers will be stored separately from the data, and only the principal investigator and the principal evaluator will have access to the identifiers.

Protection from Potential Risks

1. Although potential risks are not anticipated, project staff should adhere to the client confidentiality and protection procedures and policies to ensure the well-being of the clients.
2. Upon hiring, all project staff are required to be trained on confidentiality guidelines and are provided copies of the procedures and the code of Federal Regulations (42 CFR Part 2). Issues related to client protection and confidentiality will be discussed at least twice a year during staff training.
3. All New Horizon Association staff are trained to provide proper intervention in the event of adverse effects to participants. Additionally, they will be supervised by the agency's licensed clinical social workers, psychiatrists, and psychologists. These professional staff members are also available to provide additional care if needed.

Consent Procedures

1. Prior to acceptance into the program, clients will be informed, both in English and in their primary language, about the nature and purpose of their participation in the program and its evaluation component. Procedures that safeguard their privacy and confidentiality will be presented. The voluntary nature of their participation, their rights to withdraw from the program at anytime without prejudice, the potential risks, and the use of data collected through this project will also be discussed. Limitations on confidentiality for adolescents and court-ordered cases will be explained.
2. Informed consent will be obtained from the participants and, for clients under 18, their parents or legal guardians. Participants and their parents/guardians are required to sign a consent form prior to their enrollment into the program and an additional consent form

for participating in the evaluation. Consent forms are read to the participants and to the parents/guardians both in English and in their native language to ensure they understand the forms. Copies of the signed consent forms will be given to the participants and their parents/guardians. A copy of the sample blank consent form for this project is provided at the end of the chapter.

3. Separate consent forms will be obtained for the collection of evaluation data, in addition to the consent forms for participation in the services of the Wellness Center and the treatment program. Court-ordered individuals will also be asked to sign a separate consent form that allows the program to report their status and progress to the criminal justice personnel. Individuals not consenting to the collection of individually identifiable data for evaluative purposes will be permitted to participate in the program.

Sample Consent Forms

The following samples include consent forms for both children and adults for participating in programs and evaluation.

- Sample Program Participation Consent Form for Children and Youth (Box 7.3)
- Sample Evaluation Consent Form for Children and Youth (Box 7.4)
- Sample Program Participation Consent Form for Adults (Box 7.5)
- Sample Evaluation Consent Form for Adults (Box 7.6)

References

Derogatis, L. R. (1992). *Symptom Checklist-90-Revised.* Minneapolis, MN: NCS Pearsons.

Gelber, J., & Specter, P. D. (1987). *Psychotherapy: Portraits and fiction.* Northvale, NJ: Jason Aronson.

Gergen, K. J., & McNamee, S. (1992). *Social constructionism in therapeutic process.* London: Sage.

Germain, C. B., & Gitterman, A. (1987). Ecological perspective. In A. Minahan, et al. (Eds.), *Encyclopedia of social work* (18th ed., pp. 488–499). Silver Spring, MD: National Association of Social Workers.

Gottfredson, D. C. (1982). *Handbook for evaluating drug and alcohol prevention programs.* College Park, MD: University of Maryland, Institute of Criminal Justice and Criminology.

Hartman, A., & Laird, J. (1983). *Family centered social work practice.* New York: Free Press.

Hoffman, L. (1990). Constructing realities: An art of lenses. *Family Process, 29*(1), 1–12.

Hudson, W. (1982). Index of Self-Esteem (ISE) in *The clinical measurement package: A field manual.* Homewood, IL: Dorsey Press.

Jessor, R., & Jessor, S. (1977). *Problem behavior and psychological development: A longitudinal study of youth.* New York: Academic Press.

Meyer, C. H. (1983). *Clinical social work in the eco-systems perspective.* New York: Columbia University Press.

Pardeck, J., & Yuen, F. K. O. (Eds.). (1999). *Family health: A holistic approach to social work practice.* Westport, CT: Auburn House.

Skager, R., Fisher, D., & Maddahian, E. (1986). *A statewide survey of drug and alcohol use among California students in grade 7, 9, and 11.* Sacramento: Office of the Attorney General, Crime Prevention Center.

Von Bertalanffy, L. (1968). *General system theory.* New York: Braziller.

BOX
7.3   **SAMPLE PROGRAM PARTICIPATION CONSENT FORM FOR CHILDREN AND YOUTH**

**Project Hope
Children And Youth Program Consent**

I, _____ (print name), understand that the Project Hope is a demonstration project to improve family functioning and to prevent substance abuse related problems for children and families in City of Worthington. My parent/guardian will need to give permission for me to be in the program. I also understand that my participation is strictly voluntary and I may withdraw from any Project Hope activities at any time. Information that I share during my participation in the project is considered confidential.

I understand the rules and regulations of the project and my responsibilities with regard to the project, and I agree to abide by them. My signature below indicates my complete understanding about the Project Hope and my consent to participate in any project activities.

_____   _____   _____
(Participant's Signature)   (Date)   (Staff Name and Signature)

* * * ** * * * * ** *

I, _____ (print name), parent/guardian of _____ (print name), read and understand this consent form and give my permission for my child to participate in the aforementioned activities.

_____   _____   _____
(Parent/Guardian's Signature)   (Date)   (Staff Name and Signature)

BOX
7.4   **SAMPLE EVALUATION CONSENT FORM FOR CHILDREN AND YOUTH**

Project Hope
Children And Youth Evaluation Consent

As part of a demonstration project, New Horizon Association staff and the evaluation team will evaluate the effectiveness and benefits of the various Project Hope activities. I understand the answers that I give to the evaluators will be totally confidential. My parent/guardian will need to give permission for me to be in the program, but no one from my family and my school will see the information that I give. In addition to my information are to be grouped with others in the final report; I will be given an ID# so that I will not be identified by name in any report. However, project staff and evaluation team reserve the rights to reveal information that they have the legal mandates to report, such as child abuse and immediate danger to self and others. My participation in the project is strictly voluntary. I am free to refuse to participate or withdraw at any time. I will be asked periodically to complete questionnaires or be interviewed during and after my participation in the project.

My signature below indicates my complete understanding about the evaluation component of the Project Hope and my consent to participate in any project evaluation activities.

_____   _____   _____
(Participant's Signature)   (Date)   (Evaluator's Name and Signature)

* * * * * * * * * * *

I, _____ (print name), parent/guardian of _____ (print name), read and understand this consent form and give my permission for my child to participate in the aforementioned evaluation activities.

_____   _____   _____
(Parent/Guardian's Signature)   (Date)   (Staff Name and Signature)

BOX 7.5 SAMPLE PROGRAM PARTICIPATION CONSENT FORM FOR ADULTS

Project Hope
Program Participation Consent Form for Adults

I, _____ (print name), understand that the Project Hope is a demonstration project to improve family functioning and to prevent substance abuse related problems for children and families in the City of Worthington. I also understand that my participation is strictly voluntary and I may withdraw from any Project Hope activities at any time. Information that I share during my participation in the project is considered confidential.

I understand the rules and regulations of the project and my responsibilities with regard to the project, and I agree to abide by them. My signature below indicates my complete understanding about the Project Hope and my consent to participate in any project activities.

_____   _____   _____
(Participant's Signature)   (Date)   (Staff Name and Signature)

BOX 7.6 SAMPLE EVALUATION CONSENT FORM FOR ADULTS

Project Hope
Evaluation Consent Form for Adult Participants

As part of a demonstration project, The New Horizon Association staff and the evaluation team will evaluate the effectiveness and benefits of the various Project Hope activities. I understand the answers that I give to the evaluators will be totally confidential. No one from my family and community will see them. In addition to my information are to be grouped with others in the final report; I will be given an ID# so that I will not be identified by name in any report. However, project staff and evaluation team reserve the rights to reveal information that they have the legal mandates to report, such as child abuse and immediate danger to self and others. My participation in the project is strictly voluntary. I am free to refuse to participate or withdraw at any time. I will be asked periodically to complete questionnaires or be interviewed during and after my participation in the project.

My signature below indicates my complete understanding about the evaluation component of the Project Hope and my consent to participate in any project evaluation activities.

_____   _____   _____
(Participant's Name and Signature)   (Date)   (Staff Name and Signature)

PROGRAM PLANNING AND EVALUATION: PRACTICAL CONSIDERATIONS AND IMPLICATIONS

The practice knowledge and skills for program planning and evaluation are not static. They are dynamic, evolving, and always changing. This chapter will highlight some of these practice knowledge and know-how. Specifically, it will discuss implications of planning and evaluation for funding institutions and human service providers.

This chapter also aims to serve as a springboard for readers to start taking stock of how they can be effective and reflective practitioners. It is this ongoing self-assessment and improvement that help to improve our professional competency and service quality.

Practical Considerations and Implications for Funding Institutions

An administrator of a state human services department reflected that, when developing the Request for Proposal, she knew that it was important to explain the mission and goals of the funding opportunity, and to include a detailed description of the program application requirements. She also required program applicants to budget for and explain how the proposed programs evaluate their services. However, no details were provided in the Request for Proposal regarding the expectations and guidelines in conducting the evaluation. After reviewing many grant proposals, several programs were identified and funded. Several months into the implementation of program services, the state director still wondering, "What should I expect from programs on evaluation? How should I monitor the programs' evaluation efforts?"

When county, state, or federal departments release funds for competitive bid—or when private sources, such as foundations, provide funding for projects—program officers or program analysts are assigned to work with grantees. Program administrators and program officers of funding institutions come from a variety of backgrounds, including human services. Their knowledge and experience in program evaluation vary. They are, however, the liaisons and representatives of the funding institutions or organizations in monitoring and facilitating the service delivery efforts of programs that were granted the awards. The responsibilities of these monitors or program officers include verifying that the programs are doing what they said they were going to do (i.e., process evaluation), and assessing proper budget management. Increasingly, there is a stronger push for programs to demonstrate the differences their program services have made because of the services they offered (i.e., outcome evaluation). Program officers are not only the inspectors who audit programs, but also the advocates who help programs succeed. They are also the ones who want to have monthly statistics, quarterly summaries, annual reports, and many other types of documentation. These efforts are time consuming, tedious, and burdensome. They are, however, one of the ways to track performance and to tell the success and the human stories behind those program activities.

Program Documentation

Program staffs usually plan for their services while writing a proposal or reapplying for continued funding. They carefully list out the details including who is going to do what, when the program will begin and end, where will it occur, and who will receive the services. Hopefully, they also make plans on how they will evaluate the program. When program officers or program analysts monitor grantees, they request program staff to submit documentations that can help them determine to what extent the programs did what they said they would do. For example, program officers may look at client records that document how often did participants come to the service and what occurred when they participated. They may review roster lists or attendance sheets, they may request monthly or quarterly progress reports; or they may request other documentation that would indicate that the services were conducted and the clientele was properly served. Therefore, program staff who know what they need to document or collect at the beginning of the program year, and do so while program services are conducted, will have the documentation needed when program officers/analysts request it.

As simple as this may sound, many programs do not systematically collect this information during the time when services are delivered. They wait until the end of the program year, find out what data they need, then backtrack and try to reconstruct the information. Having a process evaluation plan at the beginning of services will allow programs to collect and document accurate information as they happen or on a regular basis (e.g., monthly). Writing quarterly and annual reports will simply be a matter of assembling the well-organized data and presenting a more vivid report of the program's successes and concerns. We all can attest to the fact that balancing your checkbook monthly and organizing your financial information neatly will make financial management and tax return time less stressful. We can also testify to the reality that that level of organization could also be wishful thinking! Urgency of other important tasks, priority changes, and possibly, just possibly, procrastination have all been the culprits. Designated responsibility, discipline, and sufficient resources for the evaluation tasks are then the important "protective factors" toward the attainments of these important recording keeping and evaluation tasks.

Expectations and Resources for Evaluation

Funding institutions continue to expect programs to evaluate their program services. Most Requests for Proposals require applicants to describe how the services being proposed will be evaluated. On the other hand, many of the funding institutions do not provide enough funding for the evaluation tasks. Funding institutions should provide clearer guidance in the Request for Proposals on how they would like programs to evaluate their programs. Do they expect a program to conduct a process evaluation, or both process and outcome evaluations? Should the programs hire outside evaluators, or can the programs conduct their own evaluation using a variety of evaluation approaches? Are the funds that can be allocated for evaluation sufficient to hire an outside evaluator? If not, how will the limited funds that can be allocated for evaluation be used? These are some of the questions funding institutions are encouraged to consider when requesting program applicants to describe how they plan to conduct an evaluation of their proposed services.

Both the funding institutions and the grantees want to evaluate and improve the services they support. The constraint, however, is that the funding resources are limited. This situation is also true for some service agencies in the implementation of evaluation. Not every agency has the resources to hire an internal or external evaluator, or has the staff who has the sufficient expertise in evaluation. If this is the case, funding institutions may consider providing the necessary resources. These may include technical assistance or training to programs so that program staff can develop the knowledge and skills needed to conduct their own internal evaluation. This is highly recommended, especially if funding institutions expect programs to conduct an outcome evaluation or impact evaluation.

Box 8.1 describes how an independently funded federal institution provides evaluation assistance to a program which is expected to conduct an outcome evaluation of services.

Program Improvement and Empowerment Evaluation

How should program officers use the evaluation results to monitor programs? Many program staffs have seen evaluation as a threat to their existence. Of those program staffs who have encountered evaluation, many see evaluation as a method for determining whether or not they will receive continued funding. If their evaluation show negative results, the chances of them losing their funding is greater than if they show positive results. While this is the reality of how funding institutions use evaluation results, evaluation can also be used to support program efforts. Program officers who monitor grant recipients could use the evaluation results as tools for program improvement. They can measure the integrity of programs by determining whether or not programs conduct a quality internal evaluation, rather than judging whether or not programs should continue because they obtain positive or negative evaluation results. Programs that have process and outcome evaluation plans demonstrate that they have an assessment system in place to examine and monitor service quality. Conducting these assessments will provide programs with information to determine if, in fact, the services were delivered; and if so, whether they were effective or not. Programs that inform their officers that their services cannot be evaluated often raise the doubts of whether or not the services were provided at all, and therefore whether the desired results were achieved.

Program officers and analysts can also use the program's evaluation results as a monitoring tool, regardless of the results obtained (i.e., positive or negative), and they can use the evaluation results for program improvement. It is important for programs to be willing to use the evaluation results to improve their services, whether or not they obtained positive or negative results. For example, if a program obtains positive outcome results, they may want to refine the quality of their services or expand services to other populations in need. If the program obtains less than positive results, the program officer could work with program staff on identifying problems, making program corrections, and monitoring progress. What program staffs do differently in light of the negative program outcomes can be the strength of the program. This is particularly true when working with new agencies, indigenous organizations, or other "developing" organizations. After all, some funding provisions are designed to support community agencies for worthy projects and to serve as a springboard for further community development.

Certainly, termination of funding is an option, if a program continues to ignore its problems and fails to make the proper corrections. The contracts that were based on the grant proposals and the evaluation data (or the lack of them) would become one of the bases for such decision.

PROJECT STAR: PROVIDING TRAINING AND EVALUATION ASSISTANCE

The Corporation for National Service (Corporation), a federal institution that allocates funds to state and local institutions/organizations for community service projects known as State and National AmeriCorps programs, expected these programs to conduct an internal outcome evaluation of their services to the community. After the first year that the Corporation instituted the State and National AmeriCorps programs, it found that program staff did not have the knowledge or skills to adhere to this request, developing and conducting an outcome evaluation of their services. Therefore, the Corporation entered into a cooperative agreement in 1995 with a research firm, Aguirre International, who developed an evaluation model using an empowerment evaluation approach, to provide evaluation assistance and training to State and National AmeriCorps programs so that they could develop the skills and conduct an outcome evaluation of services provided. The efforts of Aguirre International's training and evaluation assistance to State and National AmeriCorps programs, known as Project STAR (Support and Training for Assessing Results), provided the programs not only with the opportunity to develop the capacity to conduct an internal evaluation measuring outcomes, but also, in the process of developing evaluation plans and conducting the evaluation, provided program staff with the vehicle for improving program services.

Practical Considerations and Implications for Human Services Providers

A businessman rushed out of the airport and jumped into a taxi. He instructed the driver, "Go! Fast!" The taxi dashed out onto the highway at a high speed for about 15 minutes while the businessman was making phone calls and organizing his paperwork. Suddenly, in a panic, the businessman yelled out, "Where are you going?" The taxi driver replied, "How do I know, you only said go!"

How often do we human service providers get so involved in our busy daily work routine and end up losing sight of where we are heading or how we are doing? Having the right tools and equipment, such as the money to hire a driver to transport you in a taxi, does not necessarily mean you will be going to the right place. Having the needed professional education and the provisions of the right kinds of services are only part of the success formula. A well-developed program plan and evaluation, along with a well-coordinated program implementation, distinguish success from failure.

A commercial pilot reflected on her daily routine of flying from one city to another. She said, "We start off each trip with the front wheels of a big plane resting on a 2-by-2 foot box painted on the ground at the gate. Thousands of miles later, the front wheels stop at another 2-by-2 foot box at another gate in another city. While in flight, the plane is off course more than 90% of the time in comparison to the printed flight route. Being off course is a given, due to the ever-changing weather conditions and other considerations such as air traffic. It is, however, because of the quality planning of the original flight plan and the on-going evaluation and adjustments that are made during the flight that the plane ends up where it is supposed to be—on time and on target." How much can human service providers learn from this pilot's experience in regard to program planning and program evaluation?

Atherton and Klemmack (1982) discuss their concerns of the future of research for social workers. They recognize various important issues including: the need for a research orientation, the need for more experimentation, doing research with populations at risk, distinguishing research that serves the client or the agency, social worker or researcher, the influence of research sponsors, the need for operational definitions and specific outcome criteria, and the need for more theoretically based research. Royse, Thyer, Padgett, and Logan (2001) identify several "pragmatic issues" for program evaluation. Among them are: the political nature of evaluation, the threat of evaluation, evaluation in politically charged arenas, and cultural sensitivity issues for evaluation practice. Their comments, along with those of many writers and scholars in human services, highlight that program planning and program evaluation are both academic and professional, idealistic and pragmatic, independent and political, and most of all, an art and a science.

Do Practitioners Do Planning and Evaluation?

Human service providers from different disciplines have different degrees of training, commitment, and familiarity of program planning and evaluation. Nevertheless, many of them consider themselves as service personnel and are not interested in research and planning. They believe their main goals and functions are to provide direct service to the clients. It is the job of administrators to worry about planning and evaluation. There are also myths and speculative fears of planning and evaluation that require theory, logic, and statistics.

If social workers and other trained human service providers are satisfied with the notion that they are service technicians, then they may not have to carry too many of responsibilities of planning and evaluation. Technicians provide the important and needed support to human services, and their contributions are valuable. Being a professional, however, involves more expectations. Among them are the establishment and use of an exclusive knowledge basis, demonstration of ongoing learning and development, and self-evaluation of one's practice. The abilities and the practice of planning and evaluating one's practice and performance are both the means and characteristics of professionalism. Certainly, trained professionals are interested in improving their practices and providing better services to their client populations. It is the degree and the rigor of that involvement that separate them on the continuum of professionalism.

The Needs for Informed Planning and the Inclusion of Explanatory Studies

There are needs for identifying contributing factors and using them effectively to formulate appropriate intervention plans to address the identified problems. Exploratory and descriptive evaluation, particularly in regards to qualitative studies, provide the human faces and tell the real-life stories of the issues being studied. They provide the important process data and personal accounts that make the program planning more appropriate to the needs of the clients. They do, however, have limited power in making generalizations, and restricted confidence in making prediction and assurance of producing expected outcomes.

It is often difficult for human service providers to control their planning and evaluation environments and to incorporate very important ethical considerations. But it is still possible, and desirable, to incorporate experimental elements into the program planning and evaluation process. Use of waiting lists, interruptions due to vocation breaks such as summer holidays in schools, and staggering of service delivery schedules are among some of these methods. Single-subject designs and quasiexperimental designs are other valuable alternatives that can produce reliable data that have more explanatory power.

Diversity, Social Justice, and At-Risk Populations

The United States is a multicultural society, and human service professionals should take into consideration the existence of different cultural beliefs and practices. There is no "one size fits all," generic, and all-purpose client assessment and intervention approach that applies to all cultures. Interventions have to be refined to fit the cultural context of the particular client. Clients' perceptions and interpretations of events and issues—along with other personal, social, economic, and environmental factors—form the person-in-environment context for the formation and implementation of professional interventions. Diversity among people and cultures calls for practitioners to formulate differential and culturally appropriate interventions in working with clients of different backgrounds.

Human service professionals work with the most vulnerable populations in the society. Many of them are dealing with violence, abuse, disability, and other adverse life conditions with limited resources. Many clients come to human services at the time that their life conditions have gone beyond their normal means of coping. Minority populations face additional cultural and discrimination problems that escape the mainstream populations. Being sensitive to the diversity, social justice, and special considerations in working with at-risk populations, therefore, has to be an integral part of all program planning and evaluation processes. DuBois and Miley (1996) define social justice as "the social condition that enables all members of a society to share equally in the rights and opportunities afforded by society and in the responsibilities and obligations incurred by their membership in society" (pp. 56–57). Often, particular individuals or groups are denied of their opportunities to participate. According to DuBois and Miley, "full participation in society means that individuals have access to the social benefits of society in order to realize their own life aspirations, and, in turn, that they contribute to social well-being" (p. 57).

While advocating the uses of the strength perspective, one should also recognize the reality of problems and weakness within individuals and social systems. Among these deficiencies are the unjust social systems and human networks that deny people full participation and opportunities for betterment and actualization. Advocacy and empowerment should be inherently part of the socially responsible program planning and program evaluation.

Similar to the preventive medical health approach, an increasing number of human service professionals are focusing on detecting and addressing risk factors that may negatively affect the quality of life of clients. Risk factors relate to the individual, the family, and their environment. Children who live in families or communities where cigarette smoking is prevalent are at higher risk for the possible health damages caused by secondhand smoke. Similarly, children who live in high-crime areas have increased likelihood to be victims of crime and violence. The federal Center for Substance Abuse Prevention identifies risk factors in six different domains: individuals, peers, family, school, community, and society.

As we advocate for the use of the logic model, it represents the efforts of greater degree of standardization and the general intentions of scientific approach: study, predict, and control. As the main decision makers in the traditional social structures, the male, and particularly white male, perspectives have heavily influenced the practices of planning and evaluation. Consequently, they have set the groundwork as well as the so-called standards. With the increase of diversity in this country and the recognition of the values of diversity, there have been stronger emphases on developing program and evaluations that are inclusive and culturally competent. There are many ways to increase the diversity and competency of the planning and evaluation processes, for example:

- Employ planners and evaluators of diverse backgrounds.
- Involve the diverse target populations in the development and implementation of programs and evaluations. As we discussed earlier, empowerment is the key to respect and support diversity.
- Be sensitive to the cultural relevance of any program plan and evaluation tasks including service modality, activities, research designs, and instruments.
- Use bias free language and literatures.
- Utilize qualitative and inductive planning and evaluation approaches such as ethnographic studies.
- Maintain open-mindedness in data collection, planning, and data analysis.
- Allow culturally appropriate alterative interpretations as valid options.

Who Is the Boss?

Program planning and program evaluation are conducted for the benefits of the service recipients and that eventually lead to the well being of the community, agency, and society. The clients and their needs are the bosses and the rationale that give sanction to the program planning and evaluation processes. Human service needs that match the agency missions are the impetuses that drive the planning process, which in turn produces programs with specific interventions and activities. Program activities then drive evaluation. In reality, there may be situations in which agency programs are driven by funding rather than needs. There may be some good reasons behind a traditional mental health agency that suddenly becomes interested in getting funding to run a drunk-driver education program. However, there is also the reality of nonprofit agency's funding shortage and the increased demands for new services.

As we argue earlier, practitioners, for their knowledge and expertise in service delivery and the clients that they serve, should engage in the planning and evaluation processes. Their involvement also serves the purpose for practice evaluation that should lead to the improvement of service quality.

Due to the funding and the nature of a program, it may have an external evaluator, an internal evaluator, or a program staff and usually the program director to serve as an evaluator. There are advantages and disadvantages for having an internal or external evaluator. Nevertheless, one should bear in mind that there should be activity-driven evaluation, not evaluation-driven activities. This concern is particularly true when the outside evaluator has a higher education and apparently has more evaluation expertise.

For example, a new university professor is invited to become the program evaluator. He is interested in evaluating the program. He also wants to maintain a particular academic rigor in his evaluation design to produce fine data that he may, one day, use for possible publication. After all, he is doing this partially for meeting his community service requirements as well as scholarship activities for tenure and promotion. If there are articles coming out of these program evaluation tasks, he has met some "publish or perish" demands. Rightfully, he plans on maximizing the output of his involvement. In order to produce the academic quality data set, the program staff and participants may have to alter the program and other activities in order to produce the needed responses or data set. A simple and functional post–event debriefing may be replaced by a pre- and postexperimental design with standardized written instruments, which would first be involved in a pilot testing on a sample of the target population. Number of participants and their hours of participation may also need to be doubled in order to achieve sufficient cases for statistical analysis and enough hours or dosages to produce sufficient range of outcomes. Additionally, a comparison, and preferably a control group, could be established in a sister program.

By inviting this enthusiastic program evaluator, the program will need to make many program adjustments to accommodate the evaluation demands. At the end, the program activities are driven by the evaluation. No doubt the evaluation findings will be of great quality. In fact, if resources allow, a rigorous evaluation is always preferable. Furthermore, it is somehow in line with our support in the earlier chapters for the use of experimental designs. However, in most situations, the efforts and resources that pour into this evaluation approach may deprive the program activities, and ultimately the clients that they intend to serve. Program evaluation should be driven by activities; there should be a balance and mutual support.

Theory-Based, Objective-Guided, and Balanced Planning and Evaluation

Theory-based planning and evaluation, organized and measured by operationalized program objectives, provide the needed comprehensiveness and balance. As we proposed in Chapter 3, each program has its own philosophy or working hypothesis that is based on selected theories and practice experience. Similar to the program planning process, the evaluation process should assess the program's theory bases and use them to guide the development of evaluation.

There are process objectives, outcome objectives, and impact objectives. Program objectives should have a good mix of these three levels of objectives. Process objectives produce the needed data for reporting and other planning purposes. Outcome objectives detail the expected results and outcomes. Impact objectives extend beyond immediate gains and reach for the long-term effects. A program plan should include a balanced set of objectives that can demonstrate results at all three levels.

KISS and Develop a Buy-In

Several years ago, one of the authors (Yuen), went to an elementary school in Kansas City, Missouri, to consult on a Senior Corps program. Retired and other seniors citizens spend every day in school helping first through third grade students develop reading and study skills. It was explained to the volunteers that the principle used for planning and evaluation was KISS. The acronym stands for "Keep It Simple Stupid." Immediately, an African American woman in her 70s stood up and said, "Sir, I would appreciate it if you don't use the word 'stupid' in front of my children. How about 'sweet'?" Thanks to that nice woman, for this book KISS now stands for "Keep it Simple and Sweet." Yes, the principle is to keep the program planning and evaluation tasks simple, user friendly, practical, and easier to understand. Making these perceived complicated planning and evaluation tasks easy to use and easy to get at will increase the chances for them to be accepted and utilized. This acceptance that becomes the "buy-in" is one of the most important elements for any program planning and evaluation process. When people are involved in the process, they develop an understanding of the program and feel that they are valued. For sure, their levels of involvement increase. Although this may seem to be common knowledge, many human service providers fail to recognize its importance.

Resource Issues

The following issues are resource-related recommendations that could lead to improved incorporation of planning and evaluation:

1. Program planning and program evaluation are the integral parts of the equation of success, and should be in place from the beginning of any program. They should not be an after-thought when writing the end-of-the-year report or the continuation grant application.
2. The program manager should set aside regular time for staff and volunteers to complete planning and evaluation functions. They are part of the regular workload, not an extra burden to be conducted only after all the other tasks have been completed.
3. Similarly, there should be a sufficient budget for program evaluation. If evaluation is valued, it is to be done in a businesslike, professional manner.
4. Due to the high staff turnover rate for certain service programs, it is a good idea to have a written program plan and evaluation plan to ensure consistency.
5. Though often ignored, human resources is one of the most valuable resources that human service agencies could have. Trained and experience staff, staff who contribute, staff who work together, staff who commit to the philosophy of the program and have the expertise in service delivery are resources that make a program successful. They are capitals of the agency. The recruitment, retention, development, and management of quality staff demand the attention and support from the host organizations and the funding sources.

Summary

If you don't know where you are going, how do you know if you are going in the right direction? If you are going in the right direction, how will you know when you have arrived? Program planning and evaluation help set the course and destination.

Some people say they enjoy the journey; some say they like the destination. The truth is without either one, there is neither one! Program planning and evaluation are integral parts of any successful program, and are learned skills. Doing them well is something that needs practice. As Thomas Edison once said, "Genius is one percent inspiration and ninety nine percent perspiration." The best way to get the practice and the grant funding for service is to start doing one today! Best of luck!

References

Atherton, C., & Klemmack, D. (1982). *Research methods in social work.* Lexington: MA: D.C. Heath.

DuBois, B., & Miley, K. (1996). *Social work: An empowering profession.* Boston: Allyn & Bacon.

Royse, D., Thyer, B., Padgett, D., & Logan, T. (2001). *Program evaluation: An introduction* (3rd ed.). Belmont, CA: Brooks/Cole.

Index